emerge

the **5** most common challenges faced by middle leaders and how to overcome them

GAVIN GRIFT

Solution Tree | Press

Copyright © 2024 by Solution Tree Press

All rights reserved, including the right of reproduction of this book in whole or in part in any form.

American version published in the United States by Solution Tree Press

555 North Morton Street
Bloomington, IN 47404
800.733.6786 (toll free) / 812.336.7700
FAX: 812.336.7790

email: info@SolutionTree.com
SolutionTree.com

Printed in the United States of America

LCCN: 2024025501

Solution Tree
Jeffrey C. Jones, CEO
Edmund M. Ackerman, President

Solution Tree Press
President and Publisher: Douglas M. Rife
Associate Publishers: Todd Brakke and Kendra Slayton
Editorial Director: Laurel Hecker
Art Director: Rian Anderson
Copy Chief: Jessi Finn
Copy Editor: Miranda Addonizio
Proofreader: Sarah Ludwig
Cover Designer: Rian Anderson
Acquisitions Editors: Carol Collins and Hilary Goff
Content Development Specialist: Amy Rubenstein
Associate Editors: Sarah Ludwig and Elijah Oates
Editorial Assistant: Anne Marie Watkins

Emerge: The Five Most Common Challenges Faced by Middle Leaders and How to Overcome Them published in Australia by Grift Education. Originally published by Hawker Brownlow Education.

© 2023 by Grift Education

Acknowledgments

I would like to thank the following individuals for their support, inspiration, and guidance in the writing of this book. Colin, thank you for being my accountability coach and for always being there to help me clarify my thoughts, especially during the early stages of this book. Your support was invaluable, and I am grateful for your friendship. Clare, your valuable insights, your unwavering belief in me, and your willingness to say no when necessary helped me stay focused and committed to bringing this book to life.

Larissa and Lauren, thank you for your expertise and wisdom in editing this book. Your contributions helped shape this book into what I had envisioned. Kylie, your support of this work went above and beyond, and I appreciate all you have done to ensure that this book is of the highest quality for those who read it. Clark, thanks for your support in this work. I am excited to continue growing it with you.

To all the educators who have entrusted me to be their coach, thank you for teaching me as much as I teach you. Your dedication to the field of education is inspiring, and I am grateful to be a part of your journey.

I especially want to thank my family for their ongoing support in not only this work but also ensuring that educators around the world can benefit from the work I bring to them. Ryan, Flynn, Ella, Jude, Jo, and Mum, your sacrifices and support mean the world to me.

To Fleetwood Mac, your music was a constant source of inspiration, and I would like to thank you for giving me the motivation I needed whenever I felt stuck. Listening to your music helped me regain my focus at times and kept pushing me forward. I love the power of music, as you will see in the book!

Lastly, thanks to George, our beautiful corgi, for providing me with an excuse to leave the computer and clear my head with a good walk outside, especially during lockdown! This book is a COVID baby for sure!

With gratitude,

Gavin

Table of Contents

About the Author .... **vii**

Preface .... **ix**
My Love Affair With Teaching and Leading ix
A Leadership Dedication xi

Foreword .... **xiii**

Introduction **1**
Leadership Is Personal 1
This Book and How to Use It 4

CHAPTER 1
Clarity Precedes Competence **9**
The Importance of Clarity to Competence 9
Defining the Self-Aware Middle Leader 11
The Benefits of Self-Awareness 19
Emerge Exercises: The Self-Work 21

CHAPTER 2
Pain Points and People: Agents of Self-Awareness **23**
Seeing Hardship as an Opportunity for Growth 24
Emerge Exercises: The Self-Work 33

CHAPTER 3
Where to Focus Your Self-Awareness **35**
From Pain Point to Opportunity 35
Focusing Your Self-Awareness 37
Emerge Exercises: The Self-Work 43

CHAPTER 4
Common Pain Points for Middle Leaders **45**
Shifting Sands 45
Where to From Here? 52
Emerge Exercises: The Self-Work 53

CHAPTER 5
The Pleaser: Overcoming the Need to Be Liked **55**
Rainy Hearts 56
Emerge Exercises: The Self-Work 67

CHAPTER 6
The Ostrich: Overcoming the Overwhelm of Constant Change **69**
Rolling With It 69
Emerge Exercises: The Self-Work 84

CHAPTER 7
The Imposter: Overcoming Self-Limiting Beliefs **85**
The Voice Within 86
Emerge Exercises: The Self-Work 97

CHAPTER 8
The Dynamo: Overcoming Not Having Enough Time **99**
Slowing Down to Go Fast 100
Emerge Exercises: The Self-Work 113

CHAPTER 9
The Judge and Juror: Overcoming Difficult People at Work **117**
Taking a Different Look 118
Emerge Exercises: The Self-Work 131

EPILOGUE
Coming Into View **133**
Looking Back to Move Forward 133
A Series of Starting Lines 134

References and Resources **137**

Index **145**

About the Author

 **Gavin Grift** is the founder and CEO of Grift Education. Gavin's passion, commitment, humor, and highly engaging style have made him one of Australia's most in-demand presenters. Through his keynotes, seminars, and coaching services, Gavin connects with national and international audiences on cultivating authentic collaboration, building success in others, and genuinely committing to reflective practice. His belief in the development of defined professional autonomy for educators both challenges and connects the heads and hearts of his audiences.

Widely considered one of Australia's top authors, Gavin has a list of clients that include independent, faith-based and government education systems, high-level executives, influential corporate brands, and cutting-edge international schools. Gavin also operates a private coaching practice that focuses on empowering executive and middle leaders in their roles.

Having taught in schools and coached educators for over thirty years, Gavin understands the specific challenges educators face. He is one of Thinking Collaborative's most in-demand Cognitive Coaching Associates, having delivered the Cognitive Coaching Seminar® for fifteen years, working across three continents. He has specifically used his passion, experiences, and knowledge to design programs that assist middle leaders to overcome some of their most pressing challenges.

Gavin has become widely known as one of the most accessible and powerful education writers of today, thanks to the global impact of his bestselling books, including *Collaborative Teams That Work*, *Five Ways of Being*, *Teachers as Architects of Learning*, and *Transformative Collaboration*.

To learn more about Gavin's work, visit grifteducation.com.

Preface

Through my own journey as a leader, my increasing self-awareness has brought me fulfillment and gratitude. When I have allowed myself to be still, reflective, and honest, to take stock of where I am in my leadership mission and work out next steps, my greatest teachers always appear.

I have searched for empowerment throughout my entire life, long before I really knew what the word meant or what it represented. My leadership path has been less by design and more by chance, but it has always been propelled by a deep motivation to believe in myself and to be content in that belief. I know I'm not alone in that. I never wanted to be an author. I never wanted to be a leader. I didn't even want to be a teacher. I also didn't want to be at school.

As a student, I became self-aware very quickly to fit in, to figure out what I had to say and do to be accepted without bringing unnecessary attention to myself. Rather than being focused on learning and discovering who I could be naturally, I took the road of trying to become who I perceived others wanted or needed me to be. This started long before the tumultuous teenage years. My increasing levels of self-awareness were always clouded by placing the expectations of others above my own. I would carry this mental burden through much of my adult life and into my leadership approach. In my darkest moments, it was always my greatest teachers' belief in me that helped me overcome pain points.

My Love Affair With Teaching and Leading

I started school extremely young. I was four years old. My mum and dad probably sent me to school at this age because they didn't know what else to do with me. I was certainly a very different child at school than I was at home. My birthday was just a couple of days before the intake cut-off, and I was always the youngest in my year group. This left an indelible mark on me. The messages I received throughout my primary years, while not direct, were telling.

What we intend students to know, do, and understand is not all they learn at school. I learned a lot about myself (or at least what others thought about me) through the *hidden curriculum* (what students learn from their school experience outside of what educators intend). From my first year, and continuing through to year 5 (equivalent to about fifth or sixth grade in the United States), I learned that I was extremely quiet at school (much to the disbelief of my parents). Not through any intended curriculum, I also learned the following.

- Academically, I was very average. I was excessively shy.
- I wouldn't do well in years 11 and 12 (the last two years of high school; similar to junior and senior years in the United States) because my pen grip was a mess, which meant I wouldn't be able to write as fluently and swiftly as would be required for that level of schooling.
- I would certainly never be a writer.
- I wouldn't be as smart as my best friend Hayden. (This was based on my results on the weekly class tests and a lack of understanding of where I might have had some talent.)
- If I could help my teachers find something in me that they liked, then my days might be more pleasant.

While this is not an exhaustive list, it illustrates the power of a hidden curriculum on a student's developing self-story in their relationship with school.

A teacher by the name of Mr. Wallace shifted my narrative markedly. He looked a lot like Dennis Lillee (a famous Australian cricketer of the 1970s and -80s), although I'm sure Mr. Wallace didn't bowl as fast. At the end of each year, the principal's office would have a line of parents outside the door requesting Mr. Wallace as their child's teacher. Each December, we would sit on the outdoor basketball courts to hear who our next teacher would be, and there would be a steady stream of students muttering, "Yesssss!" as their names were read out to be in Mr. Wallace's class—it was always the same.

There were two major reasons for this. First, he genuinely cared about his students, and second, his teaching really did help all students learn. The year I was in his class shifted both my self-story and the trajectory of my life. As a result of his belief in my capabilities, his gentle but purposeful teaching manner, and his hard work and support, I came to see my friend Hayden as my academic equal and my writing (and pen grip) as more than adequate. He valued both me and the efforts I was making. He also discovered I wasn't excessively shy; in fact, I had a gift for public speaking. He even selected me for the major role as the judge in our class play, *Here Comes the Judge*.

I recall parents filing into the classroom to take their seats for the opening scene. I entered, sat in the judge's chair, opened my briefcase, and slowly started taking things out. I did this painstakingly slowly to get a reaction—and then the laughs started. I remember seeing my mum in the front row with tears rolling down her cheeks. As she looked up at me, I remember wondering why she was crying; surely, I wasn't that bad! Of course, they weren't tears of sadness. Here was her boy, who didn't say boo to a goose at school and who'd spent years developing the self-story that school wasn't a place for him, leading the school play, talking with confidence, ad-libbing, and taking center stage: a student who dared to believe that he mattered.

I fell in love with teaching that year. More to the point, I fell in love with the impact teaching can have. I wanted to do what Mr. Wallace did. It was an early discovery of the role people can play in shifting our personal self-stories through a process of empowerment. In some ways, this book started way back when that twelve-year-old boy let go of some of the limited ways he was viewing himself; he began to emerge as the person filled with possibility. This stood him in good stead as the inevitable challenges of his life path unfolded.

A Leadership Dedication

There are four leaders in my life who I dedicate this book to: (1) my first principal, Colin Sloper, who took me through the beginning thirteen years of my career as a teacher, then as an emerging and executive leader; (2) the head teacher I worked with in London for two years, Moira Arnold; (3) the business owner, visionary, and entrepreneur who gave me an opportunity to become both an author and business executive, Elaine Brownlow; and (4) my first cognitive coach, Sue Presler. As I transitioned from education into the corporate world, the roles each of these leaders played in my development were phenomenal.

They were my self-awareness levers. They told me the truth. They listened unreservedly and with kindness. They not only prevailed through hardship but also prospered. Most important, they lived their mission and stayed unapologetically true to it. They thrived because of steadfast individual beliefs in the following.

- Every student can and will learn at a high level.
- Every student deserves equal access to a quality education.

- Every educator should be able to access the best quality thinking in the advancement of education.

- True empowerment only occurs when we relinquish our biases, judgments, and need for control and give that control over to others so that they can develop power and authority over their own lives.

As leaders we must have a mission, and that mission must be an extension of what we value most, or we won't commit to it in a way that brings fulfillment and joy. When this is compromised, our truth becomes distorted, it becomes difficult to find comfort through pain, and it is too easy to be steered away from the very reason we first chose to lead. Each of these leaders exemplified this and helped me carve out the principles for my own leadership that sit at the core of this book. Their integrity mattered to me a great deal. I am indebted to each of them.

Foreword

By Kylie Lipscombe

Middle leaders are typically teachers and leaders, and they are the key brokers between senior leadership and teachers, ensuring everyone is on the same page, motivated and supported to work toward achieving the organization's vision and goals. They create a positive work culture, foster a collaborative team spirit with their colleagues, and are often the first point of contact when problems arise.

The dual role of working as and between teachers and leaders is both significant and challenging. Creating and motivating teams, gaining colleague commitment, and building shared vision in teaching and learning are important to the effectiveness of their leadership, and they are why middle leaders are commonly reported to be key influences in school improvement. However, this betweenness, often referred to as being *squeezed in the middle* or *the meat in the middle of the sandwich*, creates challenges for middle leaders as they negotiate being teachers as well as leaders. This is especially evident for new and emerging middle leaders who are moving in between the roles of teacher and leader for the first time. Reports of feelings associated with uncertainty and diffidence are rife in both research and practice as middle leaders navigate their leadership so that it does not compromise their professional selves (for example, as teachers) or personal selves.

There has been an increase in recognizing the importance of self in leadership. The idea is that effective leadership is derived not from qualifications or certification but instead from a more personal focus on an individual's understanding of their values and emotions and how these impact others, which emerges from leaders knowing and committing to themselves. The problem is that for many leaders, including middle leaders, a focus on self is difficult. Finding the time, focus, and tools to prioritize self usually comes after we prioritize students' and colleagues' needs, if at all.

Consequently, burnout, increased stress, and unproductive professional relationships can transpire.

Emerge: The Five Most Common Challenges Faced by Middle Leaders and How to Overcome Them provides readers with a rich and compelling evidence base as well as practical strategies to elevate their self-awareness and to align their beliefs and values to their actions. Ultimately, this book serves as a guide or mentor to support you to increase your impact, influence, autonomy, fulfillment, and joy and improve your relationships with others. As you read this book, you will be taken on a journey through stories, songs, humor, research, reflection, and endless tools to help you *emerge*—come forth, be known, arise—as the middle leader you want to become.

As a former middle leader and now researcher of middle leadership, I empathized, laughed, and cried, and I was both enlightened and empowered when reading this book. This much-needed resource, by a highly regarded educator and leader, shows us why middle leadership matters, and what changes we can make right now to increase our capacity to look at and after ourselves, learn and grow from difficulties, and maximize our impact when working with others.

Introduction

Open your eyes and look at the day
You'll see things in a different way

—Christine McVie

As a coach, I help middle leaders be fulfilled, influential, successful, autonomous, joyous, and connected to others through elevating their self-awareness. When you look out the leadership window, you see many things that are external to you: your colleagues, the staffroom, papers and keyboards, your mounting to-do list. When you look in the leadership mirror, you see yourself. But what do you see? What do you notice? Where does your gaze go? What feelings does it conjure up? How long can you look before turning away? *How comfortable are you with what you see? Do you like what you see? Is it enough? As you look at your leadership self, what emerges?*

Ultimately, as you look in this leadership mirror, what's hidden at this point in your journey is the reflection. When you discover whatever exists for you there, you'll find the answers to overcoming the inevitable challenges associated with living a fulfilling and fruitful leadership life.

Leadership Is Personal

I went into education to empower others. It's what others did for me. Amazing human beings helped me carve out a sense of purpose when I was searching for meaning in my professional life. We are all searching. In that search, my core mission remains the same: to find the means to help both myself and others to take control and authority over our own lives—empowerment. I am the classic example of an author writing a book to help others achieve what they themselves are striving for. After over twenty years of working in education, I want to share some insights from my search to assist others in theirs. I wrote this book specifically for middle leaders. As middle leaders, we each share common challenges, and this book is designed to assist you in overcoming them.

I was a middle leader before I had even turned thirty. I wanted to lead. I was ambitious, although I'm not exactly sure why. I suspect it was to prove to myself that I was worthy. It fueled my sense of self. I thought I knew enough about leadership; after all, I was by all accounts an accomplished teacher. As it turns out, however, I didn't know as much as I thought I did. But I wasn't aware of it at the time. I pushed forward in my endeavor to transform education, buoyed by a false confidence I had gained through listening to and believing the good things parents, students, and colleagues had to say about me.

My leadership path enabled me to wear many leadership titles: coach, network leader, acting assistant principal, leading teacher, physical education coordinator, keynote speaker, author, managing director, facilitator, presenter, and the list goes on. But title alone does not make the leader. I have hidden behind these titles when confidence was low and self-doubt was high. I have allowed my leadership ego to cloud my judgment when a clear head was needed more. I have exercised power and control in conversations with others when deep listening was what was really required. I have bought into someone else's agenda when it made me feel uncomfortable to do so—all in the name of advancement. But advancement to what? While my mission for leading is clear to me now, for a very long time, it wasn't. Once when giving a keynote, I was surprised to learn that this lack of clarity about why we lead was true for nearly all of the middle leaders I spoke to that day.

The leader within has revealed itself to me over time as my self-awareness has increased. The result of this process is insight: being able to look within and make discoveries. My hope is that this book will help you learn more about yourself and understand what you can do with these insights to help the leader within emerge.

As a young middle leader, I was heavily influenced by Stephen R. Covey's (1989) book *The Seven Habits of Highly Effective People*. I went through the process of mapping out the second habit, beginning with the end in mind, which I was really drawn to. I did the work and then shared, with anyone who cared to listen, what one could expect people would say about my character, contributions, and achievements at my funeral. The problem is, if I die writing this sentence, most of what I would want people to say about me at my funeral won't be true about me yet. The problem is not in Covey's (1989) work. If you believe in his process and apply it to your life, both deliberately and often, I have no doubt you could become very effective (however you may define it). I believe in much of what he shares in his book and have attempted, with mixed success, to incorporate a lot of that thinking into how I lead.

Leadership is not about the end point. It is about the now. It is about being clear about why we lead and then capitalizing on the power of self-awareness to fulfill our destinies as leaders through the moments that make up the paths we are on. I have seen great ideas backed by compelling evidence, rich strategies, innovative solutions, and passionate advocates turn to dust in the blink of an eye because leaders lack self-awareness in the moment. I believe that the single most important factor for finding fulfillment in our leadership lives is the ability to heighten our levels of self-awareness and use them in the present moment. After all, it's too late to use it in the past. That's been and gone. And the future—well, that hasn't happened yet.

In my experience, education places a heavy emphasis on building leadership capacity. We often see this as the panacea to giving leaders the skills to lead others so that we achieve education goals for our students. But what does *building capacity* mean? To *build* is to construct or grow. *Capacity* is how much something can contain. The idea of *building capacity* means the notion of what I refer to as enlarging the container. In essence, it's about being a lifelong learner. As we grow, so does our capacity to think, do, and express. It's only when we step outside of ourselves that we can truly understand what we do know, what we think we know (but often don't), and what we might need to know to grow. Building the capacity to be self-aware is the key to ensuring our leadership matters (to both self and others).

Leadership is personal. There is no rulebook, and we tend to lead from who we understand ourselves to be. Leadership is a privilege and a responsibility. Our thoughts, words, and deeds matter a lot to other people. People are influenced by what we do and say, whether we intend them to or not. Leadership can be scary, and it can be exciting. Leadership can be terrifying, frustrating, and fruitful—and that could all be in the same meeting or interaction!

Ultimately, though, leadership is about self-discovery. As we lead, we discover more about ourselves. And if we are willing to listen, really listen, the process of leading can be our greatest teacher. We are constantly learning about who we are in our resolve to fulfill our missions (the reasons we chose to lead in the first place). It was only five years into my middle leadership that I truly sharpened the axe on why I chose to be a leader. And to be fair, in the early days, my leadership was all about ego (my own sense of self-importance and value).

I thought if people could think in similar ways as me, do things in similar ways as me, and approach tasks in the way I did, then I was becoming an extremely effective leader. But as time marched on, I learned more about myself as a leader through an increased capacity to look at myself (to become witness to my own thoughts, deeds, and words). I gradually realized my view on leadership was narrow. My impact on others was also distorted and fed by a hungry ego that needed to know that what I was doing was making a difference.

I've had the great fortune of working with thousands of leaders from across the world through my professional development programs and books. I have also had countless formal and informal conversations with leaders, and the challenges they face resurface again and again. Many challenges center on leadership identity: how these leaders see themselves and how others see them. This creates tension as they try to deal internally with the frustrations, difficulties, and fears that a lack of clarity about leadership identity brings. Often the frustrations are a misalignment between the work they're doing and the work they want to be doing. They are often driven by a desire to grow other people, but they struggle because they work in environments in which they're feeling stifled themselves.

Nobody is really an expert on your leadership development, no matter what others might try to tell you. The only expert in leadership that matters to you is you! Our leadership is born out of the mission that we each hold deep inside. This guides us, and those whom we lead, through a process of searching for ways to achieve whatever goals we seek. And as we search, our goals change, our priorities shift, and our self-knowledge increases. It's what we do with this self-knowledge that becomes important.

This book is the result of the thousands of conversations and interactions that I've had in my twenty years in leadership. I wrote it for the sole purpose of helping the leader in you gain rich insights by elevating your self-awareness. Self-awareness is pivotal to maximizing impact and influence, enjoying a sense of autonomy, being fulfilled, and developing deeper connections with the people you lead. *Emerge* will help you clarify your mission for leading, why you lead, who you are as a leader, and what sits at the heart of the choices that you make as a leader.

This Book and How to Use It

I would like you to consider this book as being the old head on your young shoulders. I can't see you, so it doesn't matter how young you are, and you can't see me, so it doesn't matter how old I look! The point is that this book will provide you with insights from those who have traveled and are still traveling the leadership road alongside you. They are represented in this book for the sole purpose of benefiting you. If you combine the ages of those who indirectly contributed to the thinking contained in these pages, I'm sure it significantly surpasses the years you and I have been on this planet. This book is a mentor you can access anytime, anywhere, dispelling the myth that you can't put an old head on young shoulders. Whoever said that obviously doesn't know you and hasn't read this book.

As you continue to grapple with the real leadership challenges of inspiring, guiding, and creating solidarity among your peers, this book will provide you with ideas that elevate your self-awareness. You can then meaningfully examine the alignment between the beliefs and values you hold, and the behaviors and actions you enact, with the mission you have for your leadership life.

Emerge will encourage you to apply the self-knowledge gained about your ingrained dispositions, motivations, and physiological responses to move you closer to your own mission for leading. It will help to grow your emotional intelligence when leading others, ensuring your self-perceptions and behaviors are in harmony with how others see you. You'll have blind spots illuminated, and you'll be encouraged to do something valuable with what you find.

This book is informed by literally thousands of colleagues from around the world with whom I have engaged. As we continue to grapple with the universal challenges that emerge from leadership in complex and divisive times, I have been inspired by so many who turn their poisons into medicines through hard work on themselves. I have countless examples of leaders, from all walks of life and in all levels of leadership, who seek internal answers to complex external disruptions, and they teach me.

The ideas behind the messages in this book are not mine. In some cases, they date back three thousand years to philosophies that have shaped our world. They come from the voices echoed in the hallways and corridors of schools, the stories my colleagues have shared with me in our coaching sessions, and the thinking of myriad researchers, authors, practitioners, and leaders who have left lasting impressions on my consciousness. In essence, I'm not an author but rather a conduit between you and the experiences of all these people.

As you meet that leader within you with a fresh set of eyes, you will embrace the past and use the now to carve out a leadership path that takes you closer to the reasons you chose leadership in the first place.

How Will This Be Valuable?

You'll learn how to let go of some of the mental barriers associated with leadership: the need to be right, the desire to be heard over the opportunity to listen, the pressure to be inspiring and successful (however that is defined), to be all things to all people, to be constantly at your best because people are watching, and to know more than those you lead, to name just a few. You will be taken through a process of elevating your self-awareness to clarify your identity as a leader, enabling you to become more objective about what you see. You will learn to develop the leader in you who has clarity of mission and a desire to make a positive impact in the world. Your leadership ego will dissipate over the course of reading this book, and you will see things for what they really are—and therein lies possibility.

You will learn to quiet the distracting noises in your mind to move you forward on your path with a much higher sense of self, your true leadership self. You will better understand the leadership identity you are constructing for yourself in your very human need to feel a sense of value, importance, and influence. We are surrounded by and attach importance to titles. You may be a coach, a curriculum leader, a team leader, or an executive leader—and I have been all of these! You will learn how to move past these labels and toward your purposeful platform for leading.

You will emerge from your unconscious self able, with heightened self-awareness, to mitigate their potentially counterproductive powers. These can include holding false expectations (of yourself and others), judging yourself and others harshly, forsaking true collaboration for the application of your own ideas, embracing egoic listening over deep listening, and failing to truly see who the people that you are leading are.

As you emerge, you will more clearly come into view. This enables you to use your insights to increase your impact, influence, autonomy, fulfillment, and joy and to deepen your relationships with others. Use this book as your guide, as a possibility for a changed leadership life. Let it help you recognize the pain points that stop you from becoming the leader you want to be. Allow it to illuminate your deepest fears, frustrations, and challenges, and then increase your self-awareness to find the antidotes to your leadership pain points.

What Do You Mean by Finding Antidotes to Pain Points?

Antidotes are typically an external combination of ingredients that we take to combat the internal pain occurring in our body. While that's true for our physical self, from a mental perspective, it works differently. Awareness becomes the antidote for the pain point. While the pain might come from an external trigger—say, a difficult colleague, complex project, or lack of time—the antidote lies in the focus we bring to our own thinking, words, and actions, and the reasons behind these.

Use this book to discover the opportunities that often rest in your leadership self-story. The self-limiting beliefs, lack of time, challenging personalities, overwhelming responsibilities, and need to be liked can leave us feeling discontented. Let the voices I bring to this book help you unleash the potency that self-awareness can bring as you look for ways to tackle these potential trials.

The Road Ahead

The first few chapters of *Emerge* will set you up for your leadership journey. First, I will define *self-awareness* and its importance to middle leadership before digging deeper into two key enablers for developing awareness: (1) problems and (2) people. You will then discover where to focus your self-awareness to get the greatest impact from your self-work, both for yourself and for others. The remaining chapters in this book will introduce you to five archetypes, matched with real stories from my experience, to assist you in understanding the common challenges associated with leadership. I will explain practical levers designed to elevate your self-awareness to help you overcome these common pain points.

Each chapter will end with what I call *emerge exercises*—more on this at the end of chapter 1 (page 9). This will help you capture what's most important to you. I will give you practical ways to process your thinking so that possibilities come from your emergent insights. Having a journal you can use to process these exercises will help you get the most out of this book. Finally, each chapter will conclude with a quote that captures the essence of the thoughts on offer.

My goal for you is in the title: emerge. *Emergence* (n.d.) is when something comes into view; the Latin root *emergere* means "bring to light." An emergence happens when something appears where nothing was before. This book is your leadership mirror. As you observe your leadership self, you will gain clarity, illuminate blind spots, and find ways to fulfill your mission. The reflection you see will move toward you, and eventually, it will become the observer. From this vantage point, you will look back into the mirror and bear witness to the opportunities that emerge.

CHAPTER 1

Clarity Precedes Competence

*I can see clearly now the rain is gone
I can see all obstacles in my way*

—Johnny Nash

A little like the words from Johnny Nash's famous song, this chapter will support you in gaining clarity to overcome the obstacles that may appear on your leadership path. I will take you through some key concepts and words to help you understand both their meaning and their importance. So many words in education, and life itself, are used interchangeably when they have distinct differences. This is problematic when we are endeavoring to apply what we are learning or teaching others and often slows our progress.

Think about this chapter as similar to driving at night through thick fog. Imagine the dimly lit road when the fog hits and stops you in your tracks. Your heartbeat increases. Everything else slows down as your alertness rises. The visibility diminishes rapidly the further you drive, and your anxiety rises. This chapter will help you navigate hard-to-see bends in the road. As you gain clarity on the concept of self-awareness, any fog you have will lift, helping you move forward with clarity and competence.

The Importance of Clarity to Competence

Since author Mike Schmoker wrote the words from which this chapter takes its name in 2004, the importance of clarity to competence has been driven home to me (pardon the pun) in my work with schools as they endeavor to become professional learning communities (PLCs). One of the first strategies I use when working with teams in this way is think, pair, share (Harvard Graduate School of Education, 2011). First, I ask them to consider the term *professional learning community* and, without discussing, define what that term means to them. When it comes to the next part of the strategy, where we pair up and share our thinking, I ask them to look for similarities and differences between each person's definition. This is where the journey to clarity begins. As they share their responses with the whole group, I look for opportunities to highlight misconceptions and compare this thinking to the actual definition. The core reason for me taking teams through this process is to help them gain clarity about what it means to be a PLC and increase their chances of developing the competence to work in a collaborative culture.

This is important because my work with those schools is to assist them to work as a PLC, which, based on the classic definition of Richard DuFour and his colleagues (2024), my colleague Colin Sloper and I define in *Collaborative Teams That Work* as follows: "Educators committed to working collaboratively using action research in recurring collective cycles of learning to inquire into and increase the impact of their teaching practice to achieve better results for the students they serve" (Sloper & Grift, 2021, p. 2).

Essentially, my role is to provide these educators with the tools, thinking, and support to work in this way. Gaining a clear, shared understanding of what we're trying to achieve is the very first step.

There are other factors at play here too. The educators involved in this process need to trust the source of the research, feel connection in both their heads and their hearts to the concepts, and see themselves within the definition, supporting both their desire and confidence in working toward it. The critical element to all of this is gaining collective crystal clarity.

The concept of clarity preceding competence also plays out in our personal lives. I don't know about you, but I'm somebody who loves to sing (and I use the term *sing* loosely). I will sing anywhere: in the shower or in the car (mainly because I don't want to put other people's ears through the pain of hearing what comes out of my mouth) or even on my daily walk, oblivious to whom might be around as I belt out the chorus to whatever is coming from my earbuds. Having a voice that doesn't quite hit Adele's high notes isn't the worst thing. What is more troubling is when I sing a beloved song but just don't quite remember all the words, and so I have to make them up—and I know I'm not alone! This may or may not be entertaining, depending on what words I'm expelling and who's listening, but one thing is for sure. When

I know every single word of a song, I belt it out with conviction at a high volume and with greater confidence. When I'm unsure of the words, my voice softens, the intonation shifts, and a barely audible mumbling takes over. In this case, competence truly is reliant on my clarity about the lyrics.

You will be singing by the end of this chapter as we secure the first stanza, ready to explore the subsequent verses, chorus, and bridge that make up the rest of this book.

Defining the Self-Aware Middle Leader

To develop our influence and impact as middle leaders, it is important to understand the critical role self-awareness plays in our development. This becomes the platform for us to emerge from our current experiences with thoughtful clarity to excel as leaders.

Let's achieve some of that clarity now. There are myriad definitions of what constitutes a self-aware middle leader. Let's sharpen our understanding of the term *leader* to ensure we are on the same page before turning our attention to *middle leader*. Then we'll take a closer look at self-awareness and consider some important distinctions.

Leader

The root of the words *lead*, *leader*, and *leadership* is the verb *go* (Kouzes, 2009). At its core, leading is about moving forward, guiding others, and going places. Each of these definitions emphasizes the leader's position in relation to an individual or group and their final destination. This emphasis, then, gives much more weight to position than to disposition.

So, what do leaders do, and what is leadership? This depends on who is asking and who is answering, and the question again points to the complexity in the field of leadership theory. The term *leadership* has a multitude of meanings that in their own way have developed distinctive styles: the directive, facilitative, transformative, and servant leader, just to name a few. Each of these leadership styles has research to support their validity, impact, and reach. Interestingly, leadership models that are distributed (more shared, collaborative, extended, and growth focused in practice) have seen the biggest uptake in significant research since 2000 in educational settings (Gumus, Bellibas, Esen, & Gumus, 2018).

Research is converging to highlight critical and common themes in leadership theory. For example, according to Tony Bush and Derek Glover (2014) and Kenneth Leithwood, Alma Harris, and David Hopkins (2020), successful school leadership involves continuous growth, adaptability, and a willingness to reflect on and adapt practices. They find effective leaders prioritize collaboration, promote strong relationships with colleagues, and have the capacity to influence in all directions within an organization. Additionally, they propose this type of leadership involves a focus on ongoing learning and improvement as well as an emphasis on serving the needs of all staff and students.

This points toward a shift in education as we inquire into what it means for leaders to develop collaborative cultures where the growth of both self and others is critical. More autocratic leadership models that focus on position over disposition, therefore, don't seem to serve us as effectively in the technological revolution of modern times.

Middle Leader

This brings us to the impact that the term *middle* has on *leader*. Depending on where you reside in the world, middle leadership in education can also be referred to as *teacher leadership*. Focus has increased significantly on this type of leadership as a more collaborative approach to schooling has developed, resulting in greater reliance on those who sit beneath the executive level but above the rank of teacher. As pointed out by Gumus and colleagues (2018), the days of the lone, heroic leader are gone; they've been replaced by a hunger for models of leadership that promote collective performance.

Of course, it can get murky to define what the *middle* constitutes, given the vast array of studies, contexts, philosophies, and opinions people hold. The lack of clarity in the terminology used to refer to *teacher leadership* and *middle leadership* adds to this murkiness. Kylie Lipscombe, Sharon Tindall-Ford, and Jodi Lamanna (2023) state, "There is some agreement that middle leadership is distinct from teacher leadership, although there is also evidence that the boundary between these two school leadership spaces is blurred." The authors' analysis indicates that while influence is a primary focus for teacher leadership, middle leadership emphasizes relative position within the leadership hierarchy.

I find a definition offered by Jennifer York-Barr and Karen Duke (2004) helpful here. They describe *teacher leadership* as "the process by which teachers, individually and collectively, influence their colleagues, principals, and other members of school communities to improve teaching and learning practices with the aim of increased student learning and achievement" (York-Barr & Duke, 2004, pp. 287–288).

This definition picks up on some important and challenging ideas. The first is that a teacher leader sits between their responsibilities to students and their responsibilities to teachers and the principal. What's also noteworthy is the verb York-Barr and Duke (2004) offer us: *influence*.

Another scholarly definition for middle leadership offered by Peter Grootenboer, Karin Rönnerman, and Christine Edwards-Groves (2017) is "The practice of middle leading involves engaging in (simultaneous) leading and teaching by managing and facilitating educational development through collaborating and communicating to create communicative spaces for sustainable future action" (p. 248).

What strikes me about this definition (and is absent from the York-Barr and Duke [2004] definition) is that middle leaders engage in both leading and teaching at the same time. This highlights the labor-intensive nature of becoming a middle leader and the challenges inherent in occupying this space. It is clear this role requires leaders to oscillate between established and emerging professional identities.

For the purpose of this book, I offer the following contribution to how we might think about middle leadership:

> *Middle leadership is a critical position that typically combines the roles of both teaching and leading. Middle leaders are influencers of people, programs, and practices. They are the linchpins in the success of whole-school improvement. Integral to this is their work with executive leadership. They are the catalysts of collaboration among teachers and support staff, and they demonstrate strong commitment to increasing self-awareness in their personal and professional growth. They place their own and others' (both educators and students) learning at the heart of their endeavors.*

The implication is that a leader who sits between students at one end of the scale and teachers and their principal at the other has the responsibility to influence across an entire school—no easy feat. Developing the capacity to influence, both in ourselves and others, sits at the heart of this book.

The Merriam-Webster dictionary describes *influence* (n.d.) as "the power to change or affect someone or something . . . the power to cause changes without directly forcing those changes to happen." Let's digest that a little. Becoming a middle leader demands we develop the power to transform ourselves, others, and even things like policies, programs, approaches, and so on. It also assumes middle leaders will do so in a manner that isn't directly forceful, finding ways to unlock change from the inside out. And this leader could still be a full-time classroom teacher. We cannot underestimate how challenging this is, especially considering that this influence needs to affect the teaching and learning practices of colleagues and, ultimately, the learning achievement of students. These complexities are explored in research that indicates many middle leaders lack leadership experiences (Lipscombe, De Nobile, Tindall-Ford, & Grice, 2020) and don't have access to enough quality professional learning (Lipscombe et al., 2023). This is particularly troubling because we know from research that middle leaders are significantly affected by their own experiences and the contextual support they are provided (Lipscombe, Tindall-Ford, & Grootenboer, 2020).

So, what is becoming clearer? Leading from the middle is complex, and it's critical to the success of any school seeking genuine improvement in learning. The role of middle leader provides many opportunities for mental and emotional growth—and in many ways, the ultimate success of middle leaders depends on it. Building one's capacity to influence upward, sideways, and downward in a school requires a commitment to learning about how best to guide progress. Developing the capacity to navigate within the space of executive leadership and teachers is critical, as is developing the agency of teachers, fostering trusting collaborative relationships, and being accountable to both colleagues and leaders (Lipscombe et al., 2023). Middle leadership assumes a position of influence over others and a responsibility to guide them in a common mission.

The critical role middle leaders play in school improvement efforts, particularly those directly focused on improving teaching and learning practices, is indisputable. Lipscombe and colleagues (2023) go on to say:

> Middle leaders operate at the interface between different sources of influence and change within the school. While they are not responsible for the overall organisation of the schools, they are "key brokers within organisations" (Earley and Bubb, 2004, p. 162) and significant actors in distributed leadership approaches to school improvement (Lárusdóttir and O'Connor, 2017). (p. 270)

It is therefore helpful for middle leaders to consider who they might need to be to develop the practices required to traverse this complicated but important leadership path. As Amanda Sinclair (2007) puts it, a more meaningful way to think about leadership is as a form of being (with ourselves and others): "A way of thinking and acting that awakens and mobilizes people to find new, freer, and more meaningful ways of seeing, working and living. This form of leadership is anchored to personal self-awareness and mindfulness towards others" (p. 10).

Middle leadership is the first formal leadership position many teachers take, and it requires them to move from a teacher identity to a leader identity, necessitating that they shift their focus from their classroom to their whole school. This transition can create great uncertainty for middle leaders, and they may feel unsure about how to navigate their new roles and responsibilities. It can also impact their relationships with colleagues, who may begin to see and treat them differently, which can lead to a destabilization of existing support networks. This was always a genuine difficulty for me.

These challenges highlight the importance of ongoing professional development and support for middle leaders as they work to establish new identities and roles. Becoming aware of oneself and the changes occurring can have a positive impact on this transition as well. Middle leaders who take the time to reflect on their own experiences and emotions can develop a better understanding of themselves as leaders, which in turn can help them navigate challenges more effectively. Additionally, this self-awareness can enable middle leaders to build stronger relationships with colleagues while better understanding and adapting to their changing roles and responsibilities. By recognizing and embracing the shifts in their identity and relationships, middle leaders can ultimately become more effective in their leadership roles and make a positive impact on their schools.

With that in mind, let's turn our attention to understanding the concept of self-awareness.

Self-Awareness

In my fifteen years of coaching work, I've had the privilege to witness many middle leaders develop a deeper knowledge of themselves and then leverage it to increase their influence. The key to developing this self-knowledge has been increasing levels of self-awareness. So, given the importance of the concept, what do we mean by *self-awareness*, and how might it differ from being a mindful leader?

Let's start with *self*. Throughout this book, we delve into two levels to self-awareness—(1) intrapersonal (how we see ourselves, which includes conscious and unconscious layers) and (2) interpersonal (how others see us)—and explore how, through developing a greater understanding of both, we can maximize our impact, influence, and fulfillment as leaders. In their influential literature review, which focuses on defining self-awareness in the context of adult development, Julia Carden, Rebecca J. Jones, and Jonathan Passmore (2022) state, "The self is multidimensional in nature, made up of both conscious and unconscious layers (intrapersonal), and is informed by observations of others (interpersonal)" (p. 143).

There is a critical distinction that needs to be made here. In relation to the intrapersonal self that these researchers refer to, there remains one important difference relating to the role each self can play. The unconscious self cannot see what the conscious self can.

Let me elaborate. Think of the unconscious self as your ego. It's that aspect of yourself that you hear when you use the pronoun *I*. Examples might include the following.

- I am terrible when there is conflict.
- I am such a disorganized person.
- I think what she did was wrong.

This sense of self relates to the mental constructs, formed over a long period of time, that provide you with your identity. It is driven by your values (those things in life you give greatest weight to) and core beliefs (the stories about yourself that you've constructed based on your lived experiences; LePera, 2021). This unconscious self is the one that is occupied with the thoughts and emotions you recognize as your *self*. As you harness the power of self-awareness and become accustomed to witnessing your *unconscious* self, you will begin to recognize possibilities in your leadership world that previously you couldn't have even imagined—and all due to this heightened self-awareness.

I have a name for my unconscious self, helping me to develop a greater awareness of when I'm operating from my egoic state. I call my unconscious self *Klaus*, based on my Dutch heritage, to remind myself that I am not defined by my thoughts, which have developed through many years of conditioning. It helps to think of *conditioning* as the way our environments (including the society we are part of, our cultural influences, family dynamics, and other life experiences) have been deposited in us. These have formed our dispositions and propensities to think, feel, and act in certain ways, guiding our actions—and much of this is completely unconscious. As you navigate the pages of this book, my aim is to support your conscious self to emerge from your unconscious self. This will enable you to develop insights, make decisions, and commit to a leadership identity that increases your impact, autonomy, and fulfillment.

Now, to awareness. A widely accepted understanding of the word *awareness* is someone's knowledge or perception of a situation or fact. We become aware of something in the process of developing knowledge about it. Have you ever had the experience of buying a new car, and then suddenly you see that make and model everywhere? Why didn't you see that car before? Well, you did see it. But, as we know, there is a difference between seeing something and noticing something. The simple truth is, you know more about the car, it has greater meaning to you, and so you notice it more.

Carden and colleagues (2022) explain that self-awareness is anchored in our capacity to recognize how we perceive and think at both the conscious and unconscious level. It's also grounded in our ability to recognize others' feelings and our impact on them. The implication is that, through practicing self-awareness, we can better understand our feelings, thoughts, and physiological reactions and use this to drive our behaviors, monitoring the impact and influence they have on others as we do. Additionally, Tasha Eurich (2017) proposes that through strengthening our self-awareness, we have the potential to deepen both our internal (inward understanding of self) and external (understanding of how others see us) self-knowledge.

These bodies of work help us understand the role self-awareness plays in providing us with a deeper understanding of our choices and how they impact both our own lives and the lives of others. Carden and colleagues (2022) provide us with some useful thinking, summarized in the following list, to support our understanding of self-awareness.

1. Our self-awareness develops because we become aware of:
    a. What our perceptions are
    b. What our thinking is in relation to these perceptions
2. Our self-awareness increases when we improve our capacity to view our internal states from the perspective of a third person (our true conscious self).
3. Our unconscious self is simply the form our internal states have us believe is the person we are—our identity or ego.
4. Our conscious self is external to this ego form and elevates us from seeing our perceptions and thoughts as our identity to just witnessing them.
5. Being self-aware is the ability to move from the unconscious state to a conscious one.
6. A critical element to self-awareness includes our capacity to understand the impact our thoughts, deeds, and words have on others.
7. The purpose of self-awareness is threefold.
    a. To understand self
    b. To understand impact on others
    c. To understand how to use this knowledge

Some Important Distinctions

It's hard enough to gain clarity on what we would like people to understand and even more difficult to help them process that in a way that reflects what we would like them to do with it. There are two contributing factors to this issue: (1) language and (2) the reticular activating system—the nerves at the base of the brain often referred to in the cognitive coaching field as the *filter of perception* (Campbell, Halperin, & Sonuga-Barke, 2014). To assist the part of the reticular activating system, which makes sense of the world around us and the language we hear, let's distinguish among three terms that often contribute to a misunderstanding of what self-awareness means: (1) *self-knowledge*, (2) *self-consciousness*, and (3) *mindfulness*.

As I've explained in this chapter, through growing self-awareness, we develop an understanding of self (especially the unconscious self) and its impact on others. This is different from self-knowledge, which is better viewed as an outcome of developing your self-awareness. The higher your self-awareness, the deeper your knowledge of self becomes. This deeper self-knowledge provides you with an understanding of how you can positively impact both yourself and those you live, work, or play with. It's this self-knowledge that is often referred to as your personal growth and development.

Self-consciousness, on the other hand, relates to an aspect of the self-awareness process. We become more self-conscious when we can witness those internal states that form different parts of our identities, such as our thoughts, emotions, and reactions (Carden et al., 2022). Becoming more self-conscious means being able to more meaningfully witness aspects of our ego (unconscious selves) to understand their impact on the self and others. In this way, self-consciousness is a component of the self-awareness process as opposed to a synonym for it.

There are two parts to what constitutes mindfulness. One is being conscious or aware of something external—for example, being aware of someone's need for quiet while resting or keeping in mind a friend's allergies when choosing a restaurant for dinner. The second is about maintaining an in-the-moment awareness of thoughts, feelings, senses, and environment. This has its roots in Buddhist philosophy and meditation, the practice of which encourages you to embrace acceptance and pay attention to your thoughts and feelings without judgment. Building the capacity to recognize thoughts and feelings without necessarily believing that they are right or wrong—or, indeed, make up who you are—is key. They are just thoughts and emotions, coming and going with the tide of mind activity.

A commitment to becoming mindful in our leadership practices is important because it enables us to discover more about ourselves and those we lead, potentially contributing to greater success, fulfillment, and balance in both our personal and professional lives. Being mindful often is used interchangeably with developing one's self-awareness. For the purposes of this book, the key difference between mindfulness and self-awareness is the notion of acceptance and where it's applied. Being *mindful* relates to the capacity to notice thoughts and feelings in the moment through a nurturing and kind filter and then let them go to assist us to live more in the present. Learning to just accept the present moment eventuates through a process of separating our thoughts and feelings from the very essence of who we believe ourselves to be. It is what Eckhart Tolle (2004) refers to as letting go of the *egoic state*, the sense of self derived from the mental constructs that we have created for ourselves. *Self-awareness*, on the other hand, is about elevating the mind to examine those thoughts and emotions, observing their potential impact on the self and others. The distinction is that self-awareness does not necessarily center on self-acceptance or living in the present moment. In this way, becoming more self-aware may be required for mindfulness to flourish.

Consider this scenario. Jodie was working hard at becoming more effective in her facilitation of meetings. Part of this required her to ensure she kept herself and the team on task within the allocated time. To achieve this, she needed to be aware of what she was thinking and feeling as the meeting unfolded. This would help her ensure her responses furthered the goals of the team and didn't get in the way. This awareness gave her a better chance of maintaining a mindful state where she could let go of self-judgment, focus on what others were saying, and stop her mind from wandering. Masterful coaches tend to encourage the people they work with to develop mindful states so they remain present and suspend any potential bias. Self-awareness is an important aspect of developing these higher levels of mindfulness.

The Benefits of Self-Awareness

What's the benefit to increasing our self-awareness as leaders? Much has been written about the impact self-awareness can have, and many of us have personally felt the effect that insight can have on our personal and professional challenges. But it's hard because it requires us to make a commitment to work on ourselves. Often, it's easier to look out the window than in the mirror, because looking in the mirror would require us to examine our own values and beliefs and the patterns of behavior they influence. It has been said that "self-awareness is kind of like deciding to 'get real' with yourself, and then making a commitment to stay real" (Finn, 2021). If we can stay the course, the benefits are significant. A Korn Ferry Institute (2015) study of 486 companies finds a direct correlation between strong profits and higher levels of self-awareness.

There are also personal benefits to be reaped. There is growing evidence that self-awareness makes for more effective leaders (Bass & Yammarino, 1991). For example, a study of seventy-two senior executives, completed in partnership with Cornell University's School of Industrial and Labor Relations, found "a high self-awareness score was the strongest predictor of [a leader's] overall success" (Flaum, 2010, p. 5). I find Kelly Miller's (2024) research summary, in which she outlines six major benefits of self-awareness, particularly helpful.

1. **Enhanced ability to take perspective:** The assumption here is that through learning how to see ourselves in connection to others and seek perspectives from those around us, we increase our empathy and improve our relationships.
2. **Improved self-regulation:** We are more likely to respond to social norms in acceptable ways, avoiding reactions that harm the social fabric of those we work with.
3. **Increased creative achievement:** The creative process is littered with opportunities for self-awareness, and when capitalized upon, it improves our output as a result of using insights to adjust, refine, and improve.
4. **High self-esteem:** At their efficacious best, self-aware individuals can recognize the part they have played in a successful venture, fueling their self-esteem and confidence.
5. **Increased likelihood of habit change:** Genuine change in habits requires heightened levels of self-awareness. This can transform lives.
6. **Better relationships with colleagues:** Self-aware leaders enjoy better-quality relationships with their colleagues through a deep understanding of how their thoughts, emotions, and deeds impact themselves and others.

Who doesn't want some of that? When I reflect on the leadership roles I have had, I often wish that I knew then what I know now. With a greater sense of self-awareness, I believe I would have had greater impact and been less stressed. That self-awareness would have assisted me in overcoming many of the challenges associated with my role.

Leaders who cultivate their self-awareness are more likely to carve out a path that brings fulfillment, satisfaction, clarity, and success to both themselves and those they lead (Day, Fleenor, Atwater, Sturm, & McKee, 2014). These leaders also find effective ways to deal with the fallen logs, weeds, poisonous plants, and never-ending weather changes that, should they walk long and far enough, they will always encounter. They emerge armed with increasing levels of self-knowledge that bring them closer to reaching their leadership goals. They see both the challenges they face and the people they work with as opportunities for the ongoing development of their self-awareness and, ultimately, their fulfillment as leaders.

Emerge Exercises: The Self-Work

In my coaching practice, I often encourage journaling, and I give the people I work with take-home questions and exercises that relate to our sessions. They will often share feedback with me about how powerful these are in increasing their self-awareness and providing them with the chance to examine their unconscious selves in order to gain deeper meaning for themselves and others. We will replicate this process at the conclusion of each chapter in this book.

To help you get the most from your time in these pages, I will set out some prompt questions or tasks that will support you to apply the discussed strategies in your work. These are designed to encourage you to elevate your levels of self-awareness and emerge as the middle leader you aspire to be. Use these stems, questions, and exercises to capture what emerges for you in your work on self.

Consider taking the end of each chapter as an opportunity to journal about what you've learned, how you see this playing out in your leadership life, and reflections on your journey thus far. You might even like to revisit chapters from time to time and add to your initial reflections and responses in your journal.

The following exercise is designed to elevate your conscious self to help you discover the situational impact of your thinking on both yourself and others.

1. Commit to finding five minutes in your working day when you are going to bear witness to yourself. It might be leading a meeting, talking to a parent, or helping a colleague with an issue. Whatever the situation, make the decision to elevate your self-awareness.

2. Remember this involves witnessing both your unconscious self (ego) and your impact on others. Be sure to pay attention to the thoughts you have and the emotions you feel. What do you notice?

3. Record your reflections about what you have become more aware of. Ask yourself these two questions.

a. What did your thoughts and emotions tell you about yourself?

b. What impact did they have on the situation or person?

4. Based on these reflections, how might you use this knowledge in other situations or interactions?

Having carried out these steps and reflected on their outcomes, complete the following stems in your journal. These are designed to assist you in pausing, thinking, and consolidating your understanding of what this chapter has discussed and will lay the foundation for your work across the rest of this book.

- As a result of this chapter, I am clearer about . . .
- This clarity has me thinking about . . .
- Now that I know this I will . . .

At the end of each chapter, you will also find a single, summarizing question for you to reflect on. Taking the time to consider and journal about these essential questions will help you internalize the knowledge and practice discussed in the preceding chapter and, ultimately, support you to emerge as the leader you were always meant to be.

> **emerge**
>
> As a result of reading this chapter, what might you be looking forward to learning more about?

Until you make the unconscious conscious, it will direct your life and you will call it fate.

—Carl Jung

CHAPTER 2

Pain Points and People: Agents of Self-Awareness

But the struggles make me stronger
And the changes make me wise

—Cyndi Goodman & Tommy Lee James

Becoming a leader is a noble path but not an easy one. To empower others to take control and power over their own lives in their quest for living fulfilling lives is what I've always sought to achieve in my teaching and leadership life. This mission has been littered with challenges and, in some cases, significant emotional hardship. Still, these painful periods and the people they involved ultimately provided me with opportunities to develop my self-awareness. This self-awareness has enabled me to move from potential leadership disillusionment to fulfillment as my self-knowledge has grown. These challenges have taught me how to choose optimism over pessimism and self-acceptance over self-disapproval. And this is important because to be fulfilled is to be satisfied, happy, joyful, and content with what we do. Do you feel empowered as a middle leader or disempowered? Are you fulfilled as a leader or just full?

Our leadership lives ebb and flow like the tides. These tides bring us both internal and external difficulties that then become opportunities for growth, more prominent at some times and less so at others. This chapter provides you with perspectives and ideas for turning your poisons into medicine by deliberately using your deepest fears as levers for heightening your self- awareness. This will be important as you move on to later chapters, diving deeper into the most common pain points middle leaders must overcome to truly flourish. As this chapter's epigraph reminds us, challenges are inevitable, but with time and fortitude, we can grow from them.

Seeing Hardship as an Opportunity for Growth

I wouldn't be here without the exceptional people who have shown up in my life and empowered me in the truest sense of that word. My leadership path has been scattered with genuine hardship. Adversity is inevitable; it's part of life. When I became a leader, nobody told me this truth. Perhaps people don't tell us these things because they don't want to alarm us. People mean well and want to encourage leaders, not scare them away with stories of woe. But if we don't share this truth with developing leaders, we miss an opportunity to teach them about the rewards these challenges can bring.

In my work with leaders, I refer to these challenges as pain points. A *pain point* is simply a problem, frustration, or difficult issue that causes someone significant pain. It is often recurring, like an old sports injury that never fully heals. We bring our own pain points to our leadership, develop new pain points along the way, and deal with others' pain points too. While many of us try to avoid pain, the truth is that when it surfaces, at any point in our leadership lives, it can be an opportunity to grow and learn. Of course, whether we take that opportunity depends on how we focus on the pain point and what we become aware of in the process.

Any difficulty we encounter is an opportunity to bring us closer to the goals of our mission, revise our mission, or move us further away. It depends on what we become aware of, how we process it, and then what we do with it. Self-awareness is all about insight—being able to see inside of yourself—and it is crucial to living fulfilling and joyful leadership lives. Let me share some personal examples to highlight the insights that emerged from some of my leadership pain points: the role of self-awareness and how people can enable our self-awareness.

Learning From Experience

I have selected three personal experiences that represent important junctures in my journey to becoming a more self-aware leader. Each example is of a pain point from which, with deliberate observation of my unconscious self, I was able to take away critical thinking and approaches to apply in other contexts.

The Angry Parent

In my second year of teaching, I experienced my first frightening situation with a parent, Mr. X (I'll call him that because it sounds scary). Mr. X waylaid me in the corridor, literally cornered me, and accused me of picking on his child. He alleged that I had taken sides in a playground fight that had involved his son. To this day, I can recall my physiological reaction. My cheeks turned red, I couldn't talk (or think), my body shook, and my heart raced as I tried to come to terms with what was happening. It was classic shock. I apologized, scurried away, had the principal organize a meeting, and went back to class to try to pull myself together before I had to teach the next lesson.

Over time, and through genuine self-reflection with my principal, that incident taught me something important. When confronted with sudden and emerging volatile situations, I needed to focus on my breathing to remain calm, recognize what was happening in my body, and try to acknowledge what others were saying. I also learned how to offer a time later (no point chatting when your legs have turned to jelly) to genuinely hear the concerns of the other party (no matter how out of line I think they might be).

By becoming witness to my thinking, actions, and words, I could prepare myself for more effective ways of handling this type of situation in the future. It was only when I practiced self-awareness that I could learn to have useful conversations with parents in which we could focus on what was important to both of us: their children. This was another important lesson I learned from this moment in the corridor and my subsequent interactions with Mr. X. Seeking common ground is critical to fulfilling the mission of empowering others, no matter how hard the situation might seem.

The Pup I Was Sold

There have been many other challenges in my leadership life, not least of which was the boss who "sold me a pup." This saying comes from an old swindle in which somebody would be sold what was supposedly a piglet in a bag, but upon making the trade, they would find the bag instead contained a pup. (These days, many of us might be happier with the puppy!) In my situation, the pup I was sold was my new role.

I was interviewed for a middle-leader position, which meant that in a smaller Victorian primary school, I would be working as the deputy principal with a full-time teaching role (and without the remuneration). In my experience of working within the government system, the interview process was a lottery. First, you had to hope no one from the school was applying for the job, as that would often reduce your chances dramatically. While the system is set up to be based on merit and the process designed to embrace equity, it was still a human process. And often schools erred on the side of "better the devil you know."

At any rate, I have always been able to talk well, and, coupled with the fact no one else had applied, I got the job. This was momentous for me. I had been a founding member of staff in a brand-new school for over six years. I was established, well respected, and comfortable in my middle-leadership role at that time. I was too comfortable, hence my decision to apply out. So, what was the pup?

My new principal led me to believe he would support me, that he saw something in me, and that he felt it was his duty to grow my leadership capacity so that I could work toward principalship. It took me two long years to realize that support was not going to come to fruition. I had become more unhappy in my role as an educator than I had ever been. Prior to this experience, I had been fortunate to work with exceptional leaders, and I naively thought that was just how the world worked. My perception was wrong.

I ended up working for somebody who outsourced most of his grunt work to me. I worked in a school that used my passion, energy, knowledge, and desire to make a genuine difference to function at a higher level, but I wasn't getting the support I needed. I don't for a minute question this principal's intent. In fact, I believe he was oblivious to his impact on me. More importantly, I have come to understand that I had a hand in creating this situation for myself, taking on responsibilities that sat outside my jurisdiction by saying yes to things I shouldn't have. Leadership lessons abounded! It also wasn't personal—I liked my boss as a person.

Walking to the school parking lot as the sun set on another relentlessly busy day, I was upset. We had just had our first baby; sleep was limited, reserves low. Exhausted by my workload and my boss's apparent inability to see the impact of his inaction, I was at my peak of frustration and angst. It was then that my colleague, who was listening to my rant ever so patiently, said something that has always stayed with me:

> Why do you lose so much sleep over this? Isn't having a baby making you sleep deprived enough? Just remember as you toss and turn at night, [our boss] is probably sleeping soundly, not giving you a single thought. How is that working out for you?

Wow! My colleague had a way of communicating kindness with a sledgehammer—and gee, did these words strike my self-awareness with considerable impact. This conversation heralded the beginning of my ongoing leadership quest to learn to let go. It also became the catalyst for me to build some tighter boundaries around what I was willing to take on. Becoming a yes-man wasn't ultimately serving me—or others—very well.

One of the many challenges leaders face is preventing difficulties at work from contaminating other aspects of their lives. This is true for me too; I've grappled with recognizing the thoughts and emotions infecting other areas in my life so I can be more considered in how I respond. I can still see my colleague's blue Mazda drive away as I stood in the parking lot, dumbfounded by his illumination of this blind spot.

The Café Conundrum

Later in my leadership life, I became the managing director of an emerging company and suggested to one of the employees that I take her for coffee one morning. I said it would be a good time to reconnect, having sensed something shift in her interactions with me that made me feel uncomfortable. As a boss, relationships were important to me, and it felt like something wasn't right. So, we made small talk until I eventually asked her, "Can you tell me what's going on? I've noticed a difference in your responses to me lately, and it concerns me." After some awkwardness, she finally shared that she initially thought I had taken her to the café to make her position redundant. What played out in her thought processes couldn't have been further from the truth. I had wanted to reconnect because I respected and admired her work, and I knew that our relationship was important to the success of the company we both served.

I gleaned from the conversation that she had lost trust in me. I had made a flippant remark over drinks one afternoon at a conference (I couldn't even recall the remark, which is not to say it didn't happen), and she had processed it as contempt for her experience and talents. I apologized for the impact of my words on her, and I made it clear that it certainly wasn't my intent to communicate negativity, nor did I feel that way about her and her work. My apology seemed to give her courage, and she shared some other observations. I hadn't expected these, but I was open to hearing her thoughts. She mentioned I tended to cut her off when I became passionate or felt something didn't add value. That was disappointing to hear because I was trying to quash my family's trait of fighting to be heard and talking over one another—possibly a reason I was drawn to coaching. I consumed some good coffee that morning, but I walked away with something of greater value. As a leader, it's important to be willing to listen to what we might not want to hear.

If we surround ourselves with people who only tell us what we want to hear (and I noticed that became more common the higher I climbed up the leadership tree), we do a great disservice to ourselves, our people, and our organizations. All this does is feed the ego. Checking the congruence of how we see ourselves and how others see us encompasses both levels of self-awareness, and it is critical to our development as self-aware leaders. Any disconnect we may find is the opportunity to grow through heightened self-knowledge. But to make it easier for you, maybe choose to have the conversations at your favorite café—a good hit of caffeine might soften the blow.

The Role of Self-Awareness

These pain points provided me with opportunities for elevating my self-awareness. Learning from them required me to become more aware of my thoughts, emotions, and actions and also how they were contributing to the situations. To learn from them, I had to engage my conscious self. This engagement is the process of elevating self-awareness to emerge with informed choices and the potential for responding in more effective ways. Yes, I had help in doing that, but ultimately, I was left with my own thoughts and a choice about what to do with those thoughts. At times, I would examine my values and beliefs:

> *Should I stay at this school? Should I continue working with this boss? Do I believe this is how a school should operate?*

Other times I would have to examine the words I used:

> *Should I listen to my colleague? Do I really cut people off? Am I condescending? What might I do about that?*

In processing pain points, I had to consider whether my dispositions for thinking were enablers or disablers:

> *Am I being optimistic or am I coming from a place of pessimism?*

Some pain points required me to assess my physiological response to an emerging situation:

> *Is my face flushed? Is my heart racing? How can I remain calm when I'm feeling threatened?*

Some would require me to monitor others' reactions to my behavior:

> *What difference in our conversation do I notice when I seek understanding rather than being understood?*

Experiences only become lessons when we embrace the conscious self and reflect on the thoughts, deeds, and words of the unconscious self:

> *What does this experience teach me about my values, beliefs, dispositions, motivations, and physiological responses, and what does it teach me about other people?*
>
> *How might I learn from this experience to reduce frustration, fear, and difficulty and increase the chances for fulfillment and joy in the moment, both in my role as leader and in my life beyond that?*

In the following chapters, you will do this self-work.

People as Enablers of Our Self-Awareness

People are potential enablers for increasing our self-awareness, and this is especially important when we feel stuck. We come across many people in our leadership lives, and each of them can play a role in helping us to learn more about ourselves. They illuminate aspects of our leadership selves that were hidden from us before they entered our lives. Whether we use what we learn about ourselves from these is a choice. It's not how others connect with us that matters; it's how we use these interactions to shape our own leadership identities and then use that self-knowledge to increase our influence, impact, and fulfillment as leaders.

I've benefited from many people who I've worked with. Each person has helped me observe things about myself that now improve how I lead. Working with others has provided me with the opportunity to reflect on aspects of how I go about my business. We often use qualities we see in others that align with our own values and beliefs to strengthen our leadership identities.

For example, one influential leader I worked with demonstrated to me the value of embracing my inner contrarian. I often repeat the words I heard him say many times in his presentations: "You are entitled to your own opinions, but not your own facts." For me, what resonated was the notion that it's OK to disagree with something, but it will be more useful when you can base your contrary opinion on more than just your perception. I now consider this more consciously in my leadership approach because I know it was not something I did routinely even though I saw its value.

I've also had the opportunity to write and work with a colleague who stimulated my self-awareness through the lens of equity. Her resolve and commitment to influencing education policy and practices for a more accessible, just, and fair system aligned closely to my own values and beliefs. Her influence often had me wondering how I was contributing to that cause and what I might think, do, and say to promote these ideals. These were and still are important factors for me to think about as a leader who wants a better world—one where we can learn to coexist peacefully and joyfully—and sees the provision of educational opportunities for all as key to this. As a result, I am more sensitive to the different perspectives that each person brings to any interaction I have with them.

People remind us of what we believe, but beliefs aren't necessarily facts. We can gain insights about our leadership identities by interacting with other people, but it requires us to have an open mind and also the willingness to explore the ways in which their qualities align or conflict with our perceptions of self. They shine a light of awareness into our unconscious selves when we pay attention. They help us examine the beliefs and values we hold and how they connect to those of other people. When there is a disconnect between our values and theirs, rather than trying to prove ourselves right, we must use our self-awareness to develop our own self-knowledge. Therein lies our chance to grow. Therefore, let's discuss unconscious reactions and conscious responses as well as understanding differences to deepen relationships.

Unconscious Reactions and Conscious Responses

Other people are always questioning what we hold true, either overtly or covertly, and mostly without even trying. It's in the questions and statements people make, such as these.

- "Do you really think that will work?" (This usually means they value something else more.)
- "I think you're just being too sensitive." (They believe your reaction should be more like how they would have responded.)
- "You've been there too long." (They hold a different view about your job situation and the value you bring.)
- "I just don't have enough time to commit to that." (They value other things more than what you're proposing.)

These are examples of people living out their own values and beliefs (which we will explore further in chapter 3, page 35). The more aware of that you become, the greater your chance of witnessing the unconscious triggers it elicits inside of you. You can then respond with less ego. Approaching situations with an open mind, an inquiring spirit, and a respectful disposition can help you break free from your unconscious thoughts and find opportunities where you might otherwise have seen only criticism. With this open mind, inquiring spirit, and respectful disposition, you can step away from your unconscious self to see opportunity rather than possible derision. The ultimate benefit in this example could be a better working relationship.

To illustrate this point, let's consider two different responses to the first example in the list I've just given. You've just set out a course of action in a meeting. A colleague asks you, in front of the group, "Do you think that will really work?" You notice within yourself a mild anger rising.

The Unconscious-Self Reaction

Playing out an unconscious-self reaction to your colleague's question, your inner dialogue might sound something like this:

> *Don't question my experience and expertise—I've been doing this a lot longer than you.*

Your outer dialogue might then sound like this:

> *Of course I do. I've been doing it for years, and there have never been any complaints. It also saves us time and energy when we are already so busy.*

The Conscious-Self Response

Let's now think about how you might respond to that colleague's question if you take a different, more self-aware approach. Activating a conscious-self response to that same mild, rising anger, your inner dialogue might be more self-aware:

> *Careful. You're annoyed . . . assume positive intent here. My colleague may just be genuinely unsure about how to do this.*

Meanwhile, with this reflective, conscious foundation, your outer dialogue might be more considered:

> *Well, I hope it does, and it has previously, but tell me more about your concerns.*

This second scenario uses self-awareness at its most powerful. Not only do you check in on your colleague's perception of your thinking (a critical level of self-awareness), but you also provide yourself with the chance to genuinely reconcile what they say with your own values. This is an opportunity for growth. You also exhibit your growing self-knowledge by recognizing the emotional response of anger as your unconscious self, reducing the chance of an overreaction. A true taming of the ego!

This highlights the critical role people can play in revealing to us aspects of ourselves that otherwise would have stayed behind the mirror—but only when we are committed to looking.

Understanding Our Differences to Deepen Relationships

As we've explored, pain points and people are potential learning opportunities for us as leaders if we're paying attention, but they can also have a massive impact on others. When we increase our levels of self-awareness, we more knowingly understand how our own biases and ideas can impact connectedness with others. In turn, this will have you either retreat or advance in the leadership journey you have embarked on.

The teaching profession is awash with professional learning programs aimed at elevating the impact of educative efforts. The problem is everything works somewhere, but nothing works everywhere. Context matters a lot. Individual context matters most. Unless the people directly involved in a change can connect that change to their values, beliefs, thinking, actions, dispositions, and motivations, that change is headed for the scrap heap. Or at best, when the door is closed, people will just do what they have always done.

So, how do we connect those we lead to any process of change? In short, with a heightened level of self-awareness, we must tie that change to the hearts and minds of everyone involved. When this is missing, there is a disconnect between the idea and the application of that idea because the people being asked to implement change don't really want to. People need to trust that what you're saying is true. Trust comes when your thoughts, actions, and words connect with theirs. The only way of knowing is to check in—and do so often.

I have given keynotes in front of audiences of hundreds of people. I know that each of them hears the same words, observes the same gestures, watches the same slides, and even hears the same jokes (probably the same ones I used the last time they heard me speak). However, they each walk out with a different interpretation. Everyone has their own perceptual filter: their brain. What we are predisposed to think, do, and say is shaped by years of conditioning. This contributes to how our brains filter the vast amount of sensory data they are fed every second. Think now of those audience members. Why do they each walk away with different connections? It is because their confirmation bias is at play. The American Psychological Association (n.d.b) defines *confirmation bias* as "the tendency to gather evidence that confirms preexisting expectations, typically by emphasizing or pursuing supporting evidence while dismissing or failing to seek contradictory evidence."

Given the same information in my keynote, participants received different messages as their brains miss some details and generalize others. They might delete certain aspects of my presentation to make it fit with their own existing schema, which is built on their values and beliefs, thought dispositions, and personal motivations.

They may even distort what I say to help it fit their view of the world. Have you ever walked out of a meeting with a colleague and started to discuss its content, only to end up wondering whether they were really at the same meeting?

Is it any wonder that no panacea exists for the challenges of education? With so many voices, opinions, research findings, and information, what people need more than ever is for their leaders to be people they can trust. People need to trust that their work can and will connect to some aspect of how they see the world. If the cognitive dissonance is too great, they will not commit.

Within these complex challenges are our greatest opportunities. By first bearing witness to our thoughts and what they mean, we can use them to strengthen our connections with others. We can recognize what's helping and hindering in the process of connecting with others. We can understand our own biases and judgments and then learn to set them aside in our quest to forge deeper relationships with people. This growing self-awareness becomes the key ingredient to deepening our relationships with others (Takano, Sakamoto, & Tanno, 2011).

Emerge Exercises: The Self-Work

Think about someone you find difficult to lead or work with or someone you would like to get to know better, and consider the following questions.

- What are the thoughts you have in relation to this person that are potential stumbling blocks?
- What assumptions might you be making about what is important to them?
- Where might you have common ground?
- Knowing this, how might you approach this person differently, and what will you need to be on the lookout for in your own thinking to help you do this?
- What would this person notice in your actions that would signify a more effective way of working together?

In your journal, name one major pain point you currently experience in your leadership role. Be specific about what is causing you this pain.

Now respond to the following questions in your journal.

- Which of your thoughts are contributing to this pain? Which of your words are contributing to this pain?

- Which of your actions are contributing to this pain?
- As you examine your responses to these questions, how might you revise your thoughts, words, and actions to overcome this pain?
- Who might you trust to share this with to check your own perceptions and gain another perspective on your thinking?

> **emerge**
>
> As you take a step back from yourself, what might be some of the things you notice about how you unconsciously react and consciously respond to the person you identified?

Character cannot be developed in ease and quiet. Only through experience of trial and suffering can the soul be strengthened, ambition inspired, and success achieved.

—Helen Keller

CHAPTER 3

Where to Focus Your Self-Awareness

*Hey, I put some new shoes on
And suddenly everything is right*

—Jim Duguid, Matty Benbrook, & Paolo Nutini

Committing to elevating your self-awareness is all about focusing your energy in the right direction. When you make that commitment, you put on the snazzy pair of shoes that Paolo Nutini sings about; you will feel better, enjoy your surroundings, and have a more comfortable walk. In this chapter, you will take a detailed look at where you should direct your efforts in your quest to increase your self-awareness.

To use the key ideas from this book and turn them into commitments for working on yourself, it is essential to understand where you're going. After all, we all want to gain the greatest leverage from our attention and effort; there's no point putting all your time into buying the wrong pair of shoes.

From Pain Point to Opportunity

As I've mentioned, pain points can become opportunities, but only when we work on ourselves. A starting point is examining some of the areas of your leadership that you'd like to develop and some of the challenges you would like to overcome. Looking at yourself through a different lens will pay dividends when you are confronted by the common pain points associated with middle leadership. Normally, these sticking points are related to the cores of our identities, bound up in our unconscious selves—the people we believe ourselves to be, based on our thoughts, emotions, actions, and words. However, when there is so much you could focus on, where do you start? Building your awareness can help you minimize the impact of these pain points and reduce the chances of developing unproductive relationships.

To illustrate the point, let me share two stories with similar themes. Amira and Joshua were both involved in my private coaching practice, and both were grappling with self-confidence issues. Where their story is similar is that they had both applied unsuccessfully for positions of leadership that would have seen them promoted.

Joshua was feeling particularly slighted and resentful at being passed over for the job. After working at his school for ten years and being in a senior role for longer than the successful applicant, Joshua felt he was entitled to the promotion. His perception was that his experience and knowledge were superior to theirs. He also felt the interview process was not respectful of what he brought to the table. It had become very difficult for Joshua to look inward at what he might learn from this process to improve his chances of success at a future interview. Instead, he became stuck on what the selection panel, the successful applicant, and the process itself represented to him.

Contrast this with Amira's experience, and we see a very different level of self-awareness. During our coaching conversations, Amira was able to quickly focus her self-awareness on the factors she had internal control of. While she was disappointed and initially felt a dent in her confidence, we were able to identify some of the beliefs and values that she held. By understanding and accepting her thoughts and emotions in response to the decision, she was able to refine her thinking.

As in Joshua's situation, Amira's close colleague ended up winning the position. While in some ways this made it harder, it also provided her with an opportunity to grow personally. She was able to recognize her core motivations for applying for the job in the first place, which centered on influence and impact. Amira was such a passionate educator, and what she was really seeking was the opportunity to have a wider influence, to impact more people and more students. And while being passed over was a hiccup, Amira chose to not allow it to define her or her relationships.

The main difference between Joshua and Amira was what they became aware of as they engaged in the coaching process. Joshua kept his awareness on others and their roles in the outcome, while Amira used self-awareness to look at her part. Now while this doesn't mean that Joshua won't end up being promoted or finding the job of his dreams, it does mean the pain point he experienced could last longer and create other challenges. For example, it may hinder the development of his relationships, his satisfaction in the job, and his confidence in his own capacity to lead.

Focusing Your Self-Awareness

In life, there will always be external disruptions and challenges. By knowing what to focus our awareness on and heightening our self-awareness, we increase capacity to see our unconscious selves more clearly. This frees us up to depersonalize situations and outcomes (as mentioned in chapter 1, page 9), which can benefit us hugely in the long run. It can help us build better relationships, feel more satisfied in our jobs, and be less likely to take work stress home, which gets us closer to our goals.

So, where would Joshua have been better off focusing his attention, and could he have learned anything from Amira? In an analysis of thousands of studies on self-awareness, Carden and colleagues (2022) identify seven critical components to self-awareness that are important to consider when deciding where to focus our attention. I refer to these as *elements of the unconscious self*. I prefer this terminology because *element* can be defined as an essential or characteristic part of something abstract, which examining our unconscious selves certainly is.

Understanding what you observe in yourself, as well as how you see and what you notice in your unconscious self, is vital for increasing your self-awareness. By focusing on the seven elements I've highlighted, you can raise your self-awareness to develop a deeper level of self-knowledge. These seven elements are one's (1) beliefs, (2) values, (3) mental states, (4) physiological responses, (5) personality traits, (6) motivations, and (7) others' perceptions (see figure 3.1, page 38).

As figure 3.1 indicates, when we focus our attention on one or more of these elements, we illuminate what contributes to the actions of our unconscious selves. This provides us with the opportunity to examine, challenge, and shift our thinking in ways that move us closer to what we want to be doing and saying as leaders. This is due to our increased capacity to evolve our conscious selves. Through accurately and empathetically witnessing our own thoughts, feelings, and actions, we emerge with a clearer view of ourselves as leaders, offering to ourselves potential for genuine growth and development. When I refer to *growth*, I mean career progression. *Development*, on the other hand, refers to personal transformation in character, values, and mindset (human psychological changes) that improve our lives and strengthen our impact. Let's get into more detail on each element.

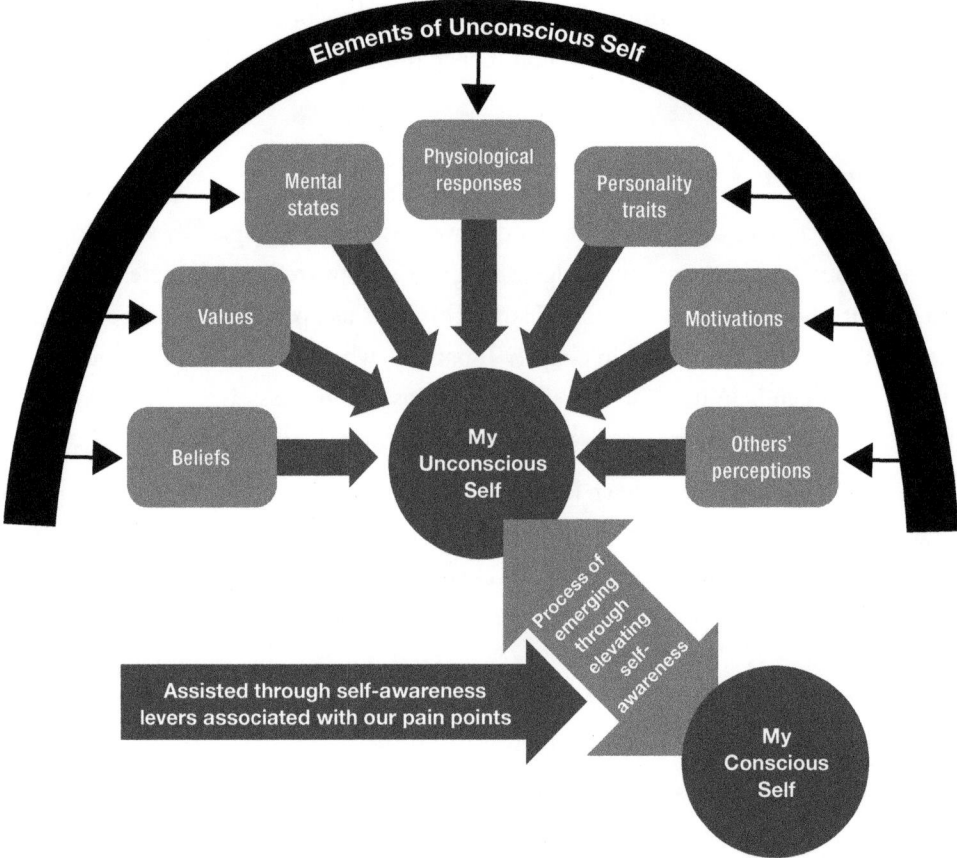

Source for elements: Carden et al., 2022.
Figure 3.1: Emerge self-awareness model.

Element 1: Beliefs

Beliefs are things we hold to be true. These beliefs are personal attitudes about ourselves and the world; they are our generalizations and are extremely personal to us (Pajares, 1992). They are based on our lived experiences and have developed over many years, which is why some people say they are hardwired. They often get confused with other labels such as *attitudes, opinions, dispositions,* and *values*. However, beliefs are the platform from which many of these other concepts take hold. For example, I have a strong belief in self-directedness, which has led me down the path of coaching people rather than evaluating them.

What's interesting about beliefs is that they don't have to be true. Beliefs are often interchanged with facts, but while they may feel true to you, it simply isn't always the case. I once believed in Santa Claus and would have argued until I was blue in the face that he was fact—until, of course, he wasn't. (I'm sorry to anyone reading this book who still believes in the big guy.) I have a belief that people will commit to things when they are able to see the benefits for themselves, but that's just a belief, not necessarily something that is true. What's a belief you hold close?

As for Joshua and Amira, the difference in their beliefs over a very similar situation could be summed up in one word: *entitlement*. Joshua believed he was entitled to the job because of his previous experience and found it extremely difficult to accept the selection panel's decision. In contrast, Amira saw missing out on this role as an opportunity to further her skills and learn more about herself, so she didn't take the knockback as hard as Joshua did.

Element 2: Values

It helps to think of values in terms of weight; the heavier the gold nugget, the more it's worth. Values are those things that we attach importance to, and we can be hierarchical about these values, prioritizing some over others. They could include being in a happy relationship, being fulfilled at work, achieving financial freedom, or living a fulfilling and autonomous life.

Because our values hold such weight, they influence the ways we think, feel, and act in any situation. I've coached many people who have developed a greater awareness of a disconnect between their own personal values and the values their schools hold, which comes to be a major pain point in their leadership.

In Joshua's and Amira's cases, they differed in their values of fulfillment and success. Because Joshua values success in his career very highly, he took a hard fall. Conversely, while Amira also wants to be successful, she values learning more than the outcome, so she was able to take the outcome in a more fruitful way.

Element 3: Internal Mental States

Depending on what you've read or experienced, you will have different ways of describing internal mental states. What I'm referring to is the thinking we do and the emotions we experience in any given situation. Sometimes *thoughts* can be defined as our cognition and *emotions* as our feelings. More specifically, *internal mental states* refer to an individual's subjective experience of their own mental and emotional processes, including their thoughts, feelings, beliefs, attitudes, and perceptions. These mental states are not observable to others, but they can influence an individual's behavior, decision making, and overall well-being.

As we learn to observe our unconscious selves, we are better able to identify the thoughts and emotions we experience in particular situations. Therein lies the opportunity for us to think differently or shift that narrative. This is a critical aspect of self-awareness because it provides us with the opportunity to detangle ourselves from ourselves—and not allow the ego to take charge. As I sit here writing, for example, my thoughts are about helping you, the reader, understand what I'd like you to do. As I examine what I'm doing right now, I notice I'm not becoming distracted, and so I am feeling calm. I'd like to say I think and feel this way every time I sit down to write a book, but sadly, this is not the case. Because I'm in the zone right now, I know it's better for me to continue working, as I'll be more productive than at other times.

It became evident to Joshua that his thoughts and emotions weren't helping him reach his ultimate goal, which was to one day become a principal. He also gradually noticed that his thoughts centered more on the unfairness of the situation and other people's role in contributing to that than on how he could learn. This included practicing his capacity to respond rather than react when feeling a high level of emotion such as resentment. Given his aim to become a principal, he also realized his responsibilities might one day increase and that he would need to understand more about processing setbacks and disappointments to work with people productively and collaboratively. Amira, on the other hand, who has a more easy-going nature, recognized that it might pay for her to spend time thinking confidently about her skill levels to present herself in interviews more convincingly. She began to understand that her relaxed way of thinking about things was often a defense deployed to prevent disappointment should things not go her way.

Element 4: Physiological Responses

We feel physiological responses to stimuli in our bodies. These bodily reactions are strongly associated with emotions; for example, if we're angry, we might go red in the face, and when stressed, we might feel a tensing of our muscles. I know I have certain triggers that result in the physiological response of a tightening in my chest. I've even felt like I'm having a heart attack before, but I wasn't—it was just my body responding to a heightened level of anxiety or fear in a moment that I lacked self-awareness. You see this in meetings all the time, say when someone starts fidgeting with their pen, swiveling in their chair, or looking into the distance. Sometimes you even see people physically squirm.

It's important to be aware of these physical responses because they are telling us to pay attention to something important. Another one of my physiological responses is the impulse to withdraw or remove myself from a situation to flee whatever feeling I'm having. The better I'm able to recognize this, the better I'm able to work through it. So, what are some physiological responses you experience that could be worth developing a higher level of self-awareness about?

In our coaching conversations, Joshua's and Amira's physiological responses were very different. Joshua's muscles tightened, he clenched his jaw, and his cheeks were very flushed as he spoke at length about the process and how he perceived it. His breathing was also shallower and more evident to me than Amira's. She was more relaxed in her body and paused for longer periods before responding to some of my questions. This indicated to me the heightened level of emotion that Joshua was trying to process.

Element 5: Personality Traits

A *trait* is a distinguishing quality or characteristic, and understanding our personality traits and becoming more aware of them is important in our leadership of ourselves and others. Myers-Briggs Type Indicators are often used in assisting people to understand their personalities. Provided they're not used as labels, they can be genuinely effective in helping people understand who they are and how they are likely to be, both by themselves and with others.

There is a vast array of resources on the subject, and, while we won't delve too deeply here, it's worth considering so we can develop a heightened level of self-awareness and allow our personality traits to become our teachers. For example, I know I am quite sensitive; I've been told even as a child this is a trait of mine. It took me years to realize it isn't necessarily a negative thing but could actually be a strength. Now that I'm more aware of this deep sensitivity, I'm able to use it in ways that benefit me and my colleagues, friends, and family without it contributing to a diminished view of self. This has only been made possible through growing my self-awareness and accepting my traits as positives. I mentioned sensitivity, but what might be one of your personality traits?

Joshua is a very loyal person, and I came to observe this as our coaching relationship developed. It was something he was also very aware of. While being an inherently good character trait, in this instance, it served as a stumbling block for moving past his feelings of resentment toward his colleague and school. Because he felt he had contributed so much and in good faith to the school community over many years, it was difficult for him to see that loyalty not repaid in kind. Meanwhile, Amira has a heavy dose of humility in her personality. This self-effacing view and diminished ego contributed to her being able to process this situation favorably. Without a heightened sense of self-importance, Amira was able to set aside some of her disappointment to process the outcome in ways that would help her the next time she applies for a job.

Element 6: Motivations

Motivations are our reasons for doing things. A greater awareness of what's driving us—why we do the things we do, feel the things we feel, and say the words we say—can be extremely helpful for developing a more mindful way of leading.

Some of the key reasons I wrote this book include my desire to empower you to take personal responsibility for your leadership life, sharing the benefits of heightening my self-awareness with others, and my enjoyment of the process of creating something from years of thinking and working in education. These reasons are important for me to focus on because they drive what I do (especially when the desire to write has temporarily left me). What are some of your motivations for reading this book?

Motivations run deep. The more Joshua and I spoke about how he was going to move forward from his disappointment, the more aware he became of some of his motivations for wanting it so badly. These went back to his upbringing. His parents did not instill in him a sense of self-belief, and they often limited his view of his potential. So, as a young adult, he developed the determination to show them he was worthy. Once he recognized this, he began challenging his own need for external validation in his quest for self-worth. Amira was energized by the process, even though she wasn't successful, because of her genuine motivation to learn. For Amira, putting herself in situations that sit outside her safety zone, regardless of the result, enables her to learn at higher levels. So, for her, the process of applying for jobs was a positive one.

Element 7: Others' Perceptions

The seventh element is about ensuring that what we view in ourselves matches how others might see us. To enhance and verify the accuracy of our self-awareness, it's important to consider what others hear and see in our words and actions and also what they think and feel about them. In essence, this element enables us to develop greater consciousness about whether the way we see ourselves is congruent with how we are seen in our wider interdependent systems of relationships. Knowledge of the perceptions of others is an important element of the unconscious self. As Eurich (2018) summarizes:

> Leaders who focus on building both internal and external self-awareness, who seek honest feedback from loving critics, and who ask *what* instead of *why* can learn to see themselves more clearly—and reap the many rewards that increased self-knowledge delivers.

Congruence in how we see ourselves and how others see us is important in the development of our own self-awareness. I can *think* I'm the most sensitive, empathetic, and approachable human being in the world. But if those I'm leading don't see me in the same way, there's a disconnect that could create pain points for everyone involved. Self-aware leaders can better leverage their own insights by checking in with others to evaluate the accuracy of their perceptions. That doesn't mean everybody finds seeking feedback from their colleagues an easy thing to do. In fact, it is a very difficult thing to do—but it is important. Of course, at times, this feedback might be given without us necessarily asking for it. Can you think of a time when someone else's perception of you didn't sit with your perception of yourself? How brave were you in seeking some understanding to learn from that disconnect?

Not surprisingly, Joshua found this element difficult. Because of the resentment that he held and the way he viewed others' contributions to the outcome, it was difficult for him to approach anybody for feedback on how he handled, processed, and acted on the decision. In essence, this element was ignored, potentially limiting his opportunity to learn more about himself. Amira, meanwhile, was open to feedback, listening to others' perceptions about what she could have done differently and what she did well. This honed her self-awareness and helped her emerge from the process better prepared for next time.

As we become more self-aware, we develop a greater level of self-knowledge. In essence, we get to know our unconscious selves more intimately. This enables us to understand better how we might think, feel, and act in certain situations. We can leverage this heightened self-awareness and make decisions, both short- and long-term, that benefit our leadership and those we lead. And, just maybe, we will be more likely to use the pain points that we will inevitably experience as opportunities to grow and develop. We'll explore the common pain points that middle leaders face in the next chapter to give you a glimpse of what opportunities might exist for you.

Emerge Exercises: The Self-Work

Using what you've learned, it's time to dig deeper into the pain point you identified in the second half of the previous emerge exercise (page 33). In your journal, answer the following questions about that particular pain point and your current practice.

- What beliefs do you hold that might be contributing to the problem? Which of your values feel compromised?
- What is your main feeling or the central narrative associated with the problem? What physiological responses have you had to the problem?

- What personality traits would be helpful to remain aware of as you navigate this problem (for example, optimism, bravery, flexibility, focus, and so on)?

- What are some of the reasons this is important to you? What do these illuminate for you?

- Who would you feel comfortable discussing your responses to these questions with? (Check with this person about whether they notice similar things. If they see things differently, what might you learn from that?)

If you found this exercise helpful, consider working through these questions again with other pain points you experience.

> **emerge**
> As you emerge from examining your unconscious self, what are you becoming more conscious of?

We have all a better guide in ourselves, if we would attend to it, than any other person can be.

—Jane Austen

CHAPTER 4

Common Pain Points for Middle Leaders

And I discovered that my castles stand
Upon pillars of salt and pillars of sand

—Chris Martin, Jonny Buckland, Guy Berryman, & Will Champion

Venturing into a life of leadership can move the ground beneath our feet. As Coldplay reminds us in the band's 2008 classic, the discovery of potential dangers and difficulties can be disconcerting, but ignoring them is even worse.

In this chapter, we will focus on what you need to elevate in your self-awareness for the greatest chance of increasing your impact, fulfillment, and well-being as a leader. We will encounter the common challenges associated with middle leadership, and I will introduce you to five archetypes that will assist you in overcoming these potential pain points. Finally, I will provide you with exercises to build your understanding of how common fears and frustrations for leaders relate to how you see yourself. This will give you the opportunity to emerge with greater self-knowledge about what might be helping and hindering your success as a leader.

Shifting Sands

As the sands around you continue to shift, this part of our book will help you stay grounded. The importance of staying grounded and how it helps middle leaders was brought home to me as I delivered Thinking Collaborative's seminars on teacher leadership. These seminars typically last two to three days and assist middle leaders with defining a leadership vision for themselves and others. Participants learn new thinking strategies and gain the tools to navigate the ongoing challenge of increasing their impact when working through change. In part, the interactions in these seminars provided the impetus to write this book.

It was on an afternoon in Adelaide, the week before COVID-19 hit Australian shores, that an emerging leader approached me on the verge of tears. She asked whether it was OK to ask for my advice on something, and of course I acceded. It was then that the floodgates opened. She asked me how to deal with resistant colleagues, unsupportive leadership, an unruly classroom, and an overwhelming sense of fatigue. She was visibly shaken. These were certainly not issues I could assist her with in such a short period, but I felt a great deal of empathy for her. Of course, I saw a connection to my own experiences in education.

We engaged in a coaching conversation, and I thought about it all the way back to the hotel and into the evening. She had hit a middle leadership nerve, one that touches so many of the issues of middle leadership. Middle leadership is a role that has feet firmly planted in two sands: (1) students and teachers and (2) senior and executive leaders. Her situation resonated not only with so many of my own experiences but also with what I was observing, reading, and hearing about.

In fact, prominent research substantiates some of my personal experiences. Studies undertaken by Martin Bassett and Nicholas Shaw (2018), Darren A. Bryant (2019), Philip Riley (2014), and Julianne A. Wenner and Todd Campbell (2017) reveal that middle leaders in education experience many limitations, including overwhelming workloads, shortage of time, administrative overload, and insufficient support. Others identify middle management in general as a minefield of incompatible norms and expectations associated with the interpersonal relationships that exist below, alongside, and above them in the organizational hierarchy (Anicich & Hirsh, 2017). This lack of clarity can lead to confusion, stress, and job dissatisfaction. These common challenges are compounded by the need to manage a wide range of relationships and build collaborative partnerships, which can involve balancing competing interests and priorities. Middle leaders may even have to alter the nature of their relationships with their peers; for example, they may have to become more formal in their approach (De Nobile, 2018). These are some compelling reasons why it's important we understand the shifts and complexities of middle leadership perhaps more than ever before (Gurr, 2019).

I decided to inquire further and, with consultation from my qualified colleagues, designed a survey to capture their dreams, their desires, their fears, and their frustrations. After more than sixty responses, many of which I found were complementary to my previous research efforts and lived experience, the patterns became evident.

I summarize these for you here with an actual quote that typifies each element of those four domains. I also provide you with the opportunity to check in on your own aspirations and challenges to compare them with the common experiences of others.

Dreams

Take a moment to consider and write down a one-sentence response to this question:

> *What are the dreams you have for your career or role?*

How did you do? Is this something you have given much conscious thought to? How does what you have written compare to the three main areas my research uncovers—(1) learning, (2) well-being, and (3) advancement?

Learning

> *To continue to push me out of my comfort zone but still provide opportunities to refine and build on existing skills and knowledge.*

This element relates to a thirst for learning and the pursuit of assisting others to learn (students and colleagues or both). Many of the responses, like this one, are about having the autonomy to make decisions that impact themselves and those they work with, to be successful in both their teaching and their leading through developing new approaches, and to generally get smarter.

Well-Being

> *To be challenged and rewarded by my work—to feel happy and balanced in my life.*

This second element is more about the relationship between respondents' personal and professional lives. The responses signal a need for a position where they can be energized, happy, effective, and valued and for this to have a reciprocal impact on their home lives. For dreams associated with well-being, healthy integration between home and work is key.

Advancement

> *I would love to be in leadership one day in the future—to lead a school to drive improvement and put my experience into practice.*

For many, becoming a more prominent leader and advancing in their career is important. The higher they climb, the more influence and learning they experience. For them, this also symbolizes success, respect, and the opportunity to be more autonomous in their decisions.

Did you pick up on some similarities? There are universal themes running through all three areas, including the need to be healthy, successful, and influential. I love the honesty of one participant's response:

> *My dreams . . . LOL. What dreams can a teacher have? Small class sizes, support for students, leadership that listens, less paperwork and politics. The list is endless.*

While the list might indeed be endless, there are things we can do to reduce its negative impact. We will get to this soon.

First, let's focus on the second question, which is about desire—which is closely related to dreams but centered more on what respondents expect their role to do for them.

Desires

Take a moment to consider and write down a one-sentence response to this question:

> *What do you want your role or career to be able to do for you?*

How did you do? Is this something you have given much conscious thought to? How does what you have written compare to the three main areas my research uncovers— (1) impact, (2) fulfillment, and (3) inspiration?

Impact

> *To feel that I am making a positive impact on the lives of students, other teachers, and families in my community.*

By far the most prominent desire these middle leaders describe is the desire to have an impact on their students and colleagues. There is an assumption that educators generally measure themselves against the benefit they bring to others, particularly in their learning. This assumption is supported by my experiences and subsequent research. We define ourselves by the difference we make; the difference we seek is both personal and contextual.

Fulfillment

> *Job satisfaction and a sense that I have successfully made a positive difference to my students.*

This element relates closely to well-being in the dreams domain. Middle leaders have a general hunger to be satisfied with what their efforts bring them. They seek joy in their work and happiness in the choices they make in their pursuit of making a difference to others so that a genuine sense of accomplishment prevails.

Inspiration

> *To energize and excite me.*

To feel energized, uplifted, and motivated in their role as teacher leaders is the third most common feature of survey responses in this field. Having chosen leadership, educators want to feel a sense of professional stimulation that provides them with the energy necessary to fulfill such a complex role.

Did you pick up on some similarities? Not surprisingly, an educator's impact sits front and center in their desire to teach and lead. One of the interesting observations is the disconnect that exists between wanting to feel inspired yet feeling overwhelmed and tired. While this can't be generalized to exist for all middle leaders, it has certainly been prevalent in the professional learning and coaching work I do with educators.

There's evidence that teachers make up to fifteen hundred decisions daily (Jackson, 1990), a number that has likely risen (Klein, 2021), so anything they can do to minimize work fatigue is surely critical to the decisions they have to make.

The third domain, fears, elaborates on this connection.

Fears

Take a moment to consider and write down a one-sentence response to this question:

> *What are the greatest sources of anxiety for you in your career or role?*

How did you do? Is this something you have given much conscious thought to? How does what you have written compare to the three main areas my research uncovers—(1) self-limiting beliefs, (2) change, and (3) relationships?

Self-Limiting Beliefs

> *Not being able to fulfill my role to the level that is required and that I expect of myself. I don't like to let others down. I fear failure in terms of not being able to deliver the outcomes as described in my role specifications.*

This element relates closely to a nagging feeling of self-doubt, which is sometimes referred to as *imposter syndrome* (a term coined to describe the fear of being exposed as a fraud; Dynamic Transitions, n.d.). These thoughts can lead to feelings of inadequacy. Leaders can spend a lot of time worrying about their credibility in the eyes of their colleagues and focusing on those colleagues' opinions. This can be coupled with a feeling of not knowing enough to do the job well. A fear of failing can also be encompassed by this element.

Change

> *I worry that I will not be able to keep up with all the current trends and technology coupled with the ever-changing expectations of our roles as educators.*

As we know, two things in life are guaranteed: death and taxes. The third thing, often not spoken about, is change. While middle leaders don't necessarily fear change itself, the process of altering and modifying in education is relentless. It can bring feelings of overwhelm leading to procrastination and distraction. (I experienced this every time I had to write student reports!) Essentially, it is a feeling of being out of control and not being able to attend to all things well because of the rapid rate of change and unforeseen deviations.

Relationships

> *Making wrong decisions that could have a detrimental effect on others and affect their trust in my ability. Speaking up to people who are "stronger" and not supportive of team goals.*

Education is relationship based, and the importance of these relationships to the outcome we seek can create great anxiety. This can range from fear of upsetting people and letting others down to disliking someone and addressing conflict. Because people are our pathway to success, the stakes are high. In my work with middle leaders, the question I get asked most often is how to work with others effectively. Remember, middle leaders sit in the center of a hierarchical structure: some are above them, while others are below. Others, of course, are beside them in the center. All of this brings unique challenges to their role.

Did you pick up on some similarities? The relationships among all three of these elements are strong. To successfully lead ourselves and others through any process of change, we need to be willing to challenge our self-limiting beliefs and find ways for the people around us to be levers for the change we seek. Easier said than done of course, but this is something the rest of this book is devoted to.

So, how do the actual hurdles we face in our work align to these deepest fears? Let's turn our attention to the frustrations many middle leaders express.

Frustrations

Take a moment to consider and write down a one-sentence response to this question:

> What are the greatest stumbling blocks to achieving your dream and desires?

How did you do? Is this something you have given much conscious thought to? How does what you have written compare to the two main areas my research uncovers—(1) time and (2) relating to others?

Time

> My biggest frustration is lack of time and the adding on of things to our workload without taking anything off. I feel my personal relationships are struggling and I just can't keep up. It is impacting my physical health.

Join in the chorus: we don't have enough . . . *time!* I have used and heard this statement more than any other over my career. But as I've learned more, I've discovered it goes beyond just a lack of time. Time is our greatest resource and one we don't want to waste in the one precious life we have been given. People understand this inherently, which is why it becomes such a source of frustration. These frustrations extend into other related areas, such as feeling the burden of a heavy workload, inadequately managing expectations, and being held hostage to the demands of others.

Relating to Others

> Meeting the needs of many different people, dealing with conflict and restorative practices, meeting expectations.

To assist in the management of time, we need productive working relationships. But the next major frustration is about how we work with and relate to the very people we need to make this happen. Issues range from working with resistant and uncommitted people to coping with people who think very differently. These issues tend to be energy suckers, leading to even greater difficulty in being able to effectively manage time.

Did you pick up on some similarities? I know that I have constantly been searching for ways to address the challenges of not having enough time and finding ways to work better with people—whether those people are higher in the leadership food chain than me or the students I've served in classrooms over the years.

As the sun set on another glorious day in Adelaide, the work to be done became clearer to me. The road that middle leaders must take to achieve their dreams and desires is built on the foundation of the very fears and frustrations they experience: their pain points. There is no panacea, but I have found some very useful approaches. First, we must become more aware of how we're confronting the very things we find challenging and identify those aspects of our unconscious selves that may be contributing to those challenges.

Where to From Here?

As Laura Baecher (2012) notes, becoming a middle leader can lead to higher levels of stress that limit their potential. Wenner and Campbell (2017) identify four critical factors that can inhibit middle leaders in their systematic review of the literature on teacher leadership. They are the following.

1. **Lack of time:** Middle leaders face an overwhelming workload that can lead to high levels of stress and burnout due to the time pressure to complete tasks.

2. **Poor relationships with peers or administrators:** Middle leaders may experience interpersonal conflicts, which can lead to stress and affect their ability to work effectively with others.

3. **Cultural and structural factors:** Middle leaders may face challenges related to organizational culture, policies, and structures, which can cause stress and negatively impact their job performance.

4. **Personal characteristics:** Middle leaders' individual traits, such as low self-efficacy or coping strategies, may make them more vulnerable to stress, which can affect their ability to perform their job effectively.

The key to not only reducing the stresses and difficulties outlined here but also using them as opportunities to grow is the development of self-awareness. This matters because when we aren't aware of the impact of our thinking, it's very difficult to move past established unhelpful patterns of behavior. Elevating self-awareness can help us move our focus from what is out of our control to what is *in* our control. This takes the emphasis off factors like the following.

- Unclear role descriptions
- Unsupportive leadership
- Lack of professional learning opportunities
- Lack of appreciation and understanding
- Not having enough time due to workload

To help you do this, over the coming chapters we will examine five archetypes (prevalent in the survey described earlier) and apply the emerge filter from chapter 3 (page 35) to each archetype. This will ensure you build the thinking, words, and deeds needed to elevate your self-awareness and increase the influence on yourself and others through your development as a leader. They will also assist you in building the personal characteristics researchers such as Wenner and Campbell (2017) identify as being critical in middle leadership roles.

I developed these five pain-point archetypes based on my own extensive experiences, research, and the countless conversations that have taken place in my coaching practice. I don't expect you to identify with them all equally. Some will be more helpful to you than others, depending on where your needs lie. But they will help you access your unconscious self to become more aware. You will also draw both comfort and strength from them as they provide you with a human map to better understand your leadership life. These archetypes represent truth and will encourage important messages to emerge in your self-guided personal work. The five pain-point archetypes, paired with their purpose in this book and your journey, are as follows.

1. **The pleaser:** Overcoming the need to be liked
2. **The ostrich:** Overcoming the overwhelm of constant change
3. **The imposter:** Overcoming self-limiting beliefs
4. **The dynamo:** Overcoming not having enough time
5. **The judge and juror:** Overcoming difficult people at work

Emerge Exercises: The Self-Work

To elevate your self-awareness of your unconscious leadership self, look over your one-sentence responses in this chapter and complete the following stems in your journal.

Beliefs

    A belief I have that moves me closer to my dream is . . .

    A belief I have that contributes to my frustrations is . . .

Values

    A value I have that moves me closer to my dream is . . .

    A value I have that contributes to my frustrations is . . .

Thoughts

    A recurring thought I have that moves me closer to my dream is . . .

    A recurring thought I have that moves me further away from my dream is . . .

Emotions

    An emotion I experience that moves me closer to my dream is . . .

    An emotion I experience that moves me further away from my dream is . . .

---

emerge

As you reflect on your responses, what do you discover about your unconscious self that is helping you? And what about your unconscious self is hindering you?

Think your way through difficulties: harsh conditions can be softened, restricted ones can be widened, and heavy ones can weigh less on those who know how to bear them.

—Stoic philosophy

CHAPTER 5

The Pleaser: Overcoming the Need to Be Liked

I don't wanna sound complaining
But you know there's always rain in my heart

—John Lennon & Paul McCartney

Everybody wants to be loved. The need for acceptance, approval, and praise from others is a natural component of being human. And while some leaders care less about their colleagues' opinions than others, everyone wants to be liked on some level. The simple fact of the matter is that there will always be individuals who dislike you, and it helps to learn to accept this. However, there is a distinction between wanting to be liked and needing to be liked.

While wanting to be liked is natural, believing that everyone must like you and then suffering worry and tension when they don't is not particularly helpful. Indeed, for many leaders, their need to be liked by everyone can become both distracting and debilitating. This has certainly been true for me in my leadership journey, and the experience has provided me with my greatest opportunities for growth.

As you read this chapter, you'll discover how being "the pleaser" plays out in your leadership. You'll also learn what to recognize to help you move beyond the risks associated with an unhelpful desire to be liked. This will include five powerful self-awareness levers for shifting your thinking. These levers will help you to remain compassionate, optimistic, and motivated, and ensure that, as you feel less of a need to be liked, you are still respected by those you lead.

Rainy Hearts

Many leaders I work with identify with the lyrics in this chapter's epigraph from the early classic Beatles song "Please Please Me." They feel depleted from putting energies into professional relationships that seem to bear no fruit and often leave them wondering, "Why don't they like me?" A pleaser wants to feel satisfied and happy, and they rely on the thoughts and opinions of others in this quest. This can result in leaders' confidence and poise being eroded, leaving them feeling blue and with a rainy heart.

However, as the saying goes, celebrate the rain, because it means that the sun shall shine bigger and brighter than ever. In this section, I'll describe my own lopsided collaboration that helped me uncover this archetype, the pleaser's pain points, and self-awareness levers to overcome these pain points.

A Lopsided Collaboration

I am an accidental author. My first book was born out of a joint passion with my coauthor for greater student agency, and the publication came about more through life circumstance than by design. This experience opened many leadership opportunities for me and took me down a different path to the one I had envisioned for my education career.

I moved from a profession in which learning was the core business to an industry in which innovation, ideas, and profit took center stage. I found the process of writing and publishing revealing on many levels, and it enlarged my frame of reference beyond what I had ever considered. It also presented new and complex challenges. This change of direction had me move in unfamiliar networks, which was both frightening and exhilarating. I encountered ego (my own as much as others') like I never had before. This whole new world magnified a significant pain point in my leadership: the need to be liked.

The pleaser in me reared its ugly head when I was involved in a significant long-term writing project with a close colleague. As the process unfolded, she continued to be unavailable when I (and the project) needed her to be available. I was proud of what we'd achieved so far, but I was growing increasingly disillusioned by her apparent lack of commitment to our work. Whether it was unanswered emails or phone calls, non-attendance at meetings, or just long periods of silence, my patience grew thin, and our collaboration suffered. I respected her intellect and considered her a friend. That made the situation harder to deal with, and it really ate away at me. I took it personally and felt she was acting in this way because she didn't have the same respect or personal regard for me. Now, that by itself wasn't the problem; it was what I recognized in my thoughts and actions (with help from my coach) that was most concerning.

Everything I did was a constant attempt to please. I was willing to do practically anything, including actions out of my usual character to engage her. This included sacrificing my own personal time and leaving too many messages and voicemails when I received no response. I was becoming a professional stalker fueled by a growing anxiety.

I suffered from the inability to stand alone or oppose her actions. I even spoke about her in a derogatory fashion to get approval and validation from others (something I pride myself on not doing). I felt I was doing all the work to maintain our professional friendship and partnership. My relentless focus on her actions was disproportionate both to my workload and to my responsibilities to others in my leadership work. My leadership heart was awash with rain.

Can you recognize any of this in yourself?

As time marched on, so did my need to act. I have seen a lot of relationship carnage in business and, to a lesser degree, in education. I didn't want our relationship to end up on the scrap heap, but something had to give. I paused (more on that later in chapter 7, page 85) and discussed it with my coach. He asked a question that struck at the heart of my self-awareness: "In what ways might you be contributing to this situation?"

As I thought about this and wrote down some of my thoughts, I noticed a pattern. I was assuming a lot of negative intent. My ego was beating a very loud drum. My self-indulgence was evident through thoughts like "I deserve better than this" and "It's not fair to me" and "I'm putting in all the effort" and "She just doesn't care about how it impacts me." It was all about me, me, me! I hadn't stopped to check in and ask if she was OK, if there was something she needed, or whether something was upsetting her. My own biases were getting in the way, and I realized it was coming from a place of pleasing, fed by insecurities and previous experiences that inhibited me from shifting my thinking from wanting to be liked to recognizing a need to be liked. I was also fueled by negative thoughts that impinged my ability to remain more neutral in my thinking. This need to be liked was leading to a lack of professional and personal boundaries that was contaminating other areas of my life.

I'm pleased to report my relationship with my colleague is now in a different, better place—and not because she did anything radically different. The main change was that I was able to express to her how I was feeling about the situation, which required me to put aside my fears of potential rejection. From this conversation, it transpired that she was being a little slack on communication because she trusted the work that I was doing and was busy with her start-up. When I understood her perspective (and realized it wasn't all about me), we managed to find a common goal in our work and organized to meet semiregularly—with our relationship intact.

I now use this elevated self-awareness in other professional relationships in my leadership life. I do not allow my ego to take over. I assume positive intent over negative intent and consciously do so. It's not perfect, but it's better. I no longer drain my own energy by thinking through all the possible implications, at times bringing out the "What do they think about me?" monologue. I challenge my thoughts (they are only temporary anyway) and minimize their tendency to impact me. I continue to try to apply what I have learned about the pleaser in me in my interactions with others, especially with those who seem to carry an extra bag of self-importance (more on this later).

My experience of working with that colleague helped me learn to manage my expectations more realistically. Sometimes we live too much within our unconscious thoughts, navel-gazing to the point where our own reality is the only thing we see. Doing this moves us further away from understanding the people we lead and love and into a world that prioritizes being liked over liking ourselves.

The Pleaser's Pain Points

The implications of always trying to impress others can be far reaching, including losing sight of your own identity and limiting the possibilities for developing your self-awareness. Understanding what truly fulfills and satisfies you as a leader is at risk. The pleaser may spend so much time attempting to please others that they lose their independence and struggle to face decisions and challenges on their own. I have experienced this myself.

Constantly pleasing others to validate one's view of oneself is very closely linked in social psychology to *sociotropy*: "a person's tendency to place an inordinate value on relationships over personal independence that will leave them vulnerable to depression in the response to a loss of relationships" (Sam, n.d.). In short, the pleaser places more value on social relationships than on their own independence—or, in the case of a leader, their professional relationships. Other debilitating consequences can follow, contributing to the frustration, tiredness, and inaction many leaders feel. Our capacity to look after ourselves and feel genuine gratitude and joy in our work can then become compromised.

Declining Self-Care

Continuously spending your time and energy to address the needs of others may cause you to lose sight of your own needs. You might find yourself becoming ill or psychologically exhausted because of the stress of attempting to satisfy everyone and everything.

Prominent thought leaders and studies have demonstrated that prioritizing the needs of others over your own self-care may result in emotional exhaustion and burnout. This is particularly true for leaders who neglect their own well-being in favor of their employees. This can cause poor performance, reduce job satisfaction, and increase turnover rates in the workplace. Additionally, people-pleasing behaviors have been associated with various negative outcomes, including anxiety, depression, and interpersonal difficulties, which can further drain a person's energy and contribute to a cycle of burnout and exhaustion (Brach, 2004; Brown, 2010; Maslow, 1943; Nagoski & Nagoski, 2019; Neff, 2011).

In my own leadership journey, this has led, on occasion, to ineffective time management, poor eating habits, lack of sleep, and heightened stress on relationships (both personal and professional). Shifting my focus from being liked by others to liking myself was my road to better self-care. This change in focus and attention to self-care is critical for middle leaders as their responsibilities increase and their role evolves to demand greater influence outside of the classroom.

Growing Resentment

Resentment can accumulate when you spend too much time putting other people first. You can find yourself repressing rage that stems from feeling that others are taking advantage of you. As a result, you may find yourself making passive-aggressive remarks or displaying other indicators of your dissatisfaction. Rather than communicating with others about what is going on and being honest about how you feel, you may begin to withdraw from them. I have seen this many times in my work helping schools to become more effective professional learning communities. Resentment erodes the collaborative culture that staff members need to address the complex challenges associated with closing the achievement gap for all students. Resentment festers.

In groundbreaking research into the role gratitude can play in overcoming resentment, Kerry Howells (2020) identifies some key consequences of harboring resentment. These include the following.

- Reduced ability to focus

- A cumulative effect that generates other resentments
- Diminished ability to see good in others
- Feelings of being a victim and blaming others
- Tendency to navel-gaze and stew on the cause of the resentment

If you think back to chapter 4 (page 45), these exact symptoms surfaced in those middle leaders' fears and frustrations.

Loss of Joy

At the other end of the sociotropy continuum is *autonomy*, which is essentially the ability of a person or group to communicate and act on their own. An unintended consequence of being a pleaser is that it becomes increasingly difficult to appreciate the innate individual pleasures associated with being a middle leader, such as those informal conversations with a member of staff or a student, or the thrill of knowing you've made a difference to someone's understanding of a subject you love.

Because of the ongoing tension that comes with committing oneself to a variety of activities and other people's perceived needs, it can become difficult to wind down, rest, and just be in the moment. This directly impacts our chances of leadership accomplishment. According to Sonja Lyubomirsky, Laura King, and Ed Diener (2005), our happiness as human beings is associated with better success and higher performance, so it pays to be satisfied with the work that we do.

From a leadership perspective, there is a genuine risk that the pleaser will develop a martyr complex, sacrificing their own values and beliefs to benefit others rather than sticking to what they hold sacred. The outcome of this sacrifice can be a debilitating loss of motivation. This can take the joy out of any efforts to lead, contribute to an erosion of genuine collaboration, and reduce the ability to delegate when necessary.

Self-Awareness Levers to Overcome the Pleaser's Pain Points

Being an excessive pleaser can yield pain points that truly hurt, so let's turn our attention to how we can elevate self-awareness and create opportunities from that pain. The five self-awareness levers we'll explore in this chapter are designed to expand your perspective so you emerge with new opportunities for growth and a greater capacity for developing mindful leadership practices.

The specific levers we explore in this chapter include the following.

1. Remember, it's not about you.

2. Consider the difference between want and need.
3. Build boundaries.
4. Move from negative to neutral.
5. Pinpoint your biases.

These levers will assist you to identify, challenge, and overcome any pleaser tendencies that you may have. Expanding your perspective can help you worry less about pleasing others, allowing you to develop stronger self-awareness and confidence in your own values and beliefs. By embracing different perspectives and ideas, you can also become more comfortable with the idea of challenging the status quo and expressing your true self without fear of judgment or rejection. No longer constrained by the need to conform to the expectations of others, this can lead to a greater sense of authenticity and fulfillment.

1. Remember, It's Not About You

In most cases, except for when we know we've overstepped or acted unprofessionally, someone else's disapproval of us reflects their character rather than our own. Often, we notice something in another person that we don't like in ourselves, and this amplifies our reaction to it. I know that was true for me in the example I gave at the start of this chapter. The reality was that my colleague's lack of commitment was something I detest in my own character—especially when other people are affected.

Focusing our attention on other people's flaws is a protective mechanism that we employ to avoid confronting the less-than-pleasant aspects of our own personalities. This can be experienced when someone first meets us and makes a hasty judgment before even getting to know us. When we have healthy self-esteem and feel confident in our own skin, we are less likely to engage in this behavior ourselves.

There is something decidedly unique about being human. No matter how hard we try to live our lives in peace and connection with others, we inevitably say and do things that upset people. We know the difference between intentionally and unintentionally doing this, but either way, it doesn't feel nourishing. We make mistakes. While we have control over what comes out of our lips and what we toss in the direction of others, we have no control over how our words and actions affect them. Each individual views the world through the lens of their own unique life experiences—their filters of perception. What may turn off one individual may appeal to another.

What is most critical is our intent. We choose the intent behind our thoughts and actions. As middle leaders, these intentions should be centered on the mission, values, and goals of your organization alongside your pursuit of others' learning and development. It is then entirely up to others how they choose to process and act on your intentions.

This in no way diminishes our responsibility for the well-being and performance of others, but it does go a long way to ensuring the pleaser in you doesn't sabotage your efforts to lead with conviction, integrity, and purpose.

2. Consider the Difference Between Want and Need

There is a difference between wanting to be liked and needing to be liked. In the situation I described earlier, I had an overwhelming desire to be liked. I wanted my coauthor to recognize my talents, commitment, and output. But did I really *need* to be liked? As I've said, it is natural for human beings to want to be liked; however, the belief that everyone must like us will often lead to suffering through the heightened worry and anxiety generated by fear—the fear of being disliked. As middle leaders, this can be a distraction from work, sap our energy, and lead to overthinking.

To feel liked is to feel validated, so it stands to reason that the less external validation we seek, the less we feel the need to be liked—even though we may still want to be (it certainly feels better than not being liked). When we are not liked, it feels like rejection, exclusion. It makes us feel different, which is obviously unpleasant. This takes us away from feeling accepted, like we are part of something, fit in, and belong to a group. This is the greatest form of relatedness, so it's critically important to our motivations and engagement in our role as educators (Lyubomirsky et al., 2005).

For many people, being unpopular is uncomfortable and sometimes distressing, but we can learn new patterns of thinking to eventually overcome it. This is more of a pain point for some leaders, depending on their social conditioning. It's a battle I've fought throughout my leadership journey, and I've worked hard to resist the urge to choose being liked over being respected and impactful. But, as you can see, it's not an easy task, which is one of the reasons the situation with my colleague lasted years, not months. This is important to note because our leadership journey is one of emergence, in which we learn about ourselves and use self-awareness to shift the internal narratives that might be getting in our way over time.

However, for many middle leaders I have coached, the instant they sense there is a chance someone may not find them amusing, supportive, agreeable, or likeable, winning them over becomes their core mission. The prospect of someone disliking them causes them to feel as though their leadership is at stake, and they become fearful. This leads to attempts to obtain attention, favor, or acceptance, often bringing about the opposite consequence.

It pays for middle leaders to accept the fundamental human desire to be liked—but only when they couple it with an ability to let go of the need to be liked.

3. Build Boundaries

Boundaries divide and separate—whether it be the sideline of a football field that determines when a ball is in or out of play, or an established nighttime routine that includes no technology an hour before bedtime. Middle leaders benefit from applying the concept of boundaries to their relationships with other people, including what they consider acceptable or inappropriate professional behaviors. In essence, it's about understanding our limits as leaders.

Recognizing our limits (where we draw the line) typically results from a principled sense of self-worth. In this context, *self-worth* refers to the validation of oneself, independent of other people or their attitudes toward us. This sense of self-worth is critical to building boundaries that reduce the chances of the pleaser within surfacing at unhelpful moments. A middle leader will benefit from having a clear understanding—and an acceptance in others—of the following categories of boundaries: emotional, cognitive, personal, and time.

Emotional Boundaries

How you feel in relation to particular people, things, and situations is your right, but it is also your responsibility to acknowledge the same right in others and the impact your emotions may have.

Cognitive Boundaries

Your thoughts, opinions, and perspectives are a right, but you also have the responsibility to respect those of others, particularly in pursuit of the broader goal of your team or school.

Personal Boundaries

Your personal life is your own business, as it is for your colleagues. Constant commentary on the personal lives of others within a professional context can be extremely damaging to the building of relational trust.

Time Boundaries

Time management is completely within your control (more on this later). Where do you draw the line in relation to what you will do with your professional time based on the expected time commitments associated with your role? I understand this is not easy, but the more time you give, the more people will take. It may also pay for you to set more realistic expectations in relation to what you expect from others. Thinking about how everyone is grappling with demands on their time can help us take a more empathetic stance.

Identifying our boundaries can be challenging. It is even harder to implement them with fidelity. (I have been trying, unsuccessfully, to reduce my cheese intake for years given my elevated cholesterol.) It can be helpful to think about people you admire for the boundaries they hold true to. What do you notice about how they communicate with others that you could learn from? What do they do? Could you learn from the emotional, cognitive, personal, and time boundaries of any other people?

4. Move From Negative to Neutral

"It is what it is!" You've probably heard this many times, or even uttered it yourself. While this statement can be grating, it does beautifully encapsulate the concept of neutral thinking. This is a mindset in which you accept both the good and the bad. At its core is acceptance. Rather than dwelling on the negative aspects of a difficult past or a physical or mental struggle, you simply accept what has occurred as reality—and then try your hardest to move on. Practicing my capacity to think neutrally has been critical to my growth as a cognitive coach, assisting me to suspend any bias or judgment and be truly present for those I work with.

I struggled majorly with this aspect of my thinking in the situation with the noncommittal coauthor I described at the start of this chapter. Every action she took (or didn't take, as the case was), I processed negatively: "She doesn't care," "I'm not important to her," and so on. As time went on and my self-awareness increased, so did my capacity for accepting what *was* without attaching negative or positive connotations to the situation. By embracing more of a neutral stance in my thinking, I was able to let go of the negativity and more successfully move forward in my work. I did this by making fewer judgments of myself as situations arose. Accepting things as neither good nor bad but just as they are sits at the heart of neutral thinking (Moawad, 2020). You can try to apply neutral thinking by, instead of thinking negatively ("I'm having such a bad day") or wishfully ("Why can't they just . . ."), accepting things just as they are.

This is not to say that there aren't obvious benefits to thinking positively or even, at times, negatively (it sometimes pays to be cynical). However, when we learn to also think from a neutral perspective, we can better navigate the complex and uncertain terrain of having to influence upward, sideways, and downward as a middle leader.

Developing your ability to think impartially, where you don't feel the push and pull of the pressure associated with so many issues you face, can have a freeing effect. Being free from negative self-talk and its associated feelings can help you live more presently. This enables you to benefit from a heightened level of self-awareness where the conscious self notices the unconscious self and frees it from the restrictions such negativity can bring. This in turn reduces the desire to feel the constant need to please others.

5. Pinpoint Your Biases

Often referred to as our personal blind spots, our unconscious biases shape how we feel and think about others. They are deeply woven into our unconscious selves and have major implications for the pleaser. This is closely linked in sociology to the concept of personal *habitus*, which is defined as "the way society becomes deposited in persons in the form of lasting dispositions, or trained capacities and structured propensities to think, feel, and act in determinant ways, which then guide them" (Wacquant, 2005, p. 316, as cited in Navarro, 2006, p. 16).

This may be why we find it difficult to see our biases in the first place, as they have formed in our unconscious selves over a long period of time and through vast amounts of social conditioning. When we couple that with the challenges of leading and working with people who have had their own distinct forms of social conditioning, it is no wonder we experience moments where we think, "I didn't see that coming!" So, what can we do about it?

It is helpful to understand that our biases come in a variety of forms. Several of the most pervasive relate to individuals' perceptions about their own thinking habits in comparison with those of others and how preconceptions of others influence how we see (or don't see) others. These biases can result in unhelpful stereotyping, unenlightened presumptions, and potential discriminatory practices.

In our context, unconscious biases can typically be categorized as confirmation, affinity, attribution, and conformity bias. I've summarized these different forms as described in the work of Bailey Reiners (2023).

- *Confirmation bias* is the tendency to form opinions about a situation or a person based on your own wishes, beliefs, and prejudices rather than objective merit.
- *Affinity bias*, sometimes referred to as *similarity bias*, refers to people's tendency to associate with those who share similar interests, experiences, and backgrounds.

- *Attribution bias* is a psychological phenomenon in which you seek to make sense of or criticize another person's behavior based on your previous observations and interactions with them.
- *Conformity bias*, sometimes referred to as *peer pressure*, is the tendency for people to behave similarly to others around them, regardless of their own unique views or idiosyncrasies (this bias can be very prevalent in the approach of the pleaser).

Increasing your awareness of the potential unconscious biases you hold can be useful in broadening your impact as a leader. We all have unconscious biases, so where might the possibilities lie for you as you pinpoint where yours lay?

Use the following simple self-assessment to increase your awareness of your biases and think about how they both help and hinder your work in overcoming the challenges associated with being a pleaser. Consider each of the four biases and corresponding statements set out in figure 5.1 and note which point on each scale reflects your current practice. The higher the number, the more prevalent the bias may be in your thinking.

Having used figure 5.1 to evaluate the presence of these biases in your current practice, consider how these biases might be contributing to your need to be liked and then respond to the following question:

> How might increasing your awareness of your personal biases help you address or overcome your need to be liked?

In this chapter, we have taken a deep dive into the implications of being a pleaser. We have not only identified some of the consequences of operating from the perspective of needing to be liked, but we have also explored five self-awareness levers to help you move forward. The following emerge exercises will help you to make the most of the opportunities offered by your growing self-awareness.

I have designed these exercises to avoid overwhelming you with possibilities or encouraging you to commit to so much that you become paralyzed into inaction. Feeling overwhelmed can be a natural part of embarking on any substantial change and have us running to bury our heads in the sand like ostriches. We will dig further into this potential pain point in chapter 6 (page 69), which covers the archetype of the ostrich and discusses overcoming the overwhelm of constant change.

Confirmation bias				
In my need to be liked, I form opinions about a situation or a person based on my own wishes, beliefs, and prejudices rather than on objective merit.				
1	2	3	4	5
Never	Rarely	Sometimes	Often	Always
Affinity bias				
In my need to be liked, I have a tendency to associate with those who share similar interests, experiences, and backgrounds as me.				
1	2	3	4	5
Never	Rarely	Sometimes	Often	Always
Attribution bias				
In my need to be liked, I seek to make sense of or criticize another person's behavior based on my previous observations and interactions with them.				
1	2	3	4	5
Never	Rarely	Sometimes	Often	Always
Conformity bias				
In my need to be liked, I tend to behave similarly to others around me, regardless of my own unique views or idiosyncrasies.				
1	2	3	4	5
Never	Rarely	Sometimes	Often	Always

Figure 5.1: Pinpointing biases tool.

Emerge Exercises: The Self-Work

Let's dig deeper into the pain points associated with being the pleaser. Use these questions to capture what has emerged for you in your work on self and what you might do with that knowledge. Take your time to record your responses and thinking in your journal.

- In what situations will it be important for you to remember, "It's not about you"?
- When might it assist you to apply the mantra, "It's great to be liked, but I don't need to be liked"?
- What can you build a clear boundary around to assist you in overcoming the need to be liked? (You might like to record this as a complete statement: "I am going to build a clear boundary around . . .")

- Who will you look to for assistance in building that clear boundary?
- In what situation (or, with which person) could it be helpful to reform your negative thoughts into more neutral thinking?
- What are the facts (proof that it is true) about the situation or person? What are your thoughts about those facts (not necessarily true)?
- What might you need to let go of to neutralize your thinking about this?

> **emerge**
>
> As you reflect on your responses to these questions and commitments, what are you becoming more conscious of? How might this become an opportunity for you?

Being unafraid of not being liked is the best way to be liked.

—Inès de La Fressange

CHAPTER 6

The Ostrich: Overcoming the Overwhelm of Constant Change

When life is too much, roll with it, baby . . .
Hard times knocking on your door

—Steve Winwood, Will Jennings, Brian Holland,
Lamont Dozier, & Eddie Holland

As a middle leader constantly facing change, I repeated one mantra to myself many times: this too shall pass. Change fatigue is as real as it is common. Developing the capacity to roll with the inevitable changes associated with leading from the middle requires the ability to move forward with purpose, even under the relentless pressures of a demanding job. As musician Steve Winwood mentions in his 1980s hit, hard times will come knocking—and as a middle leader, change can be the cause of these hard times. This can make the job exhilarating but also potentially overwhelming at the same time.

Rolling With It

Think back to chapter 1 (page 9), where I discussed the distinct role middle leaders play in influencing upward, influencing sideways, and influencing downward. The role of a middle leader is multifaceted and complex, and it is far too common to feel the weight of classroom, team, and whole-school responsibilities. This weight can be crushing, exacerbated by a sense of overload triggered by relentless rates of change and the inherent challenges associated with educating young people.

This can create in each of us a propensity to revert to what I refer to as *the ostrich* archetype. In order to survive, we bury our heads in the sand and hope it will all go away, waiting until it is safe to re-emerge. In short, we embrace the coping mechanism of avoidance. "This too shall pass" becomes a way of being.

In my school-based leadership experiences, I knew the ostrich was alive and well in me when internal narratives like these cropped up.

- The principal will eventually leave.
- There's only one term to go.
- I can change schools or departments next year.
- The holidays are just around the corner.
- Just focus on the students and ignore everyone else.
- It's just the same thing dressed up differently.
- I've heard all this before.

These inner stories were littered with cynicism, fatigue, and skepticism. They were all about survival, and they indicated my resources were low, my energy depleted, and my mindset fixed.

As you might expect, the ostrich experiences many pain points. I will elaborate on these in this chapter, but key is that focus is taken away from the work demanded of middle leaders. The good news is we can learn to overcome the sense of overwhelm central to the ostrich's plight and develop habits that make the ostrich less likely to appear. This is how we learn to roll with it—not by ignoring the cause of discomfort but by becoming more self-aware of how our unconscious selves may be contributing to the problem.

Importantly, an ostrich doesn't really put its head in the sand in the way we might imagine; it simply digs deeper into the sand to check on its eggs when facing impending danger. It is a temporary and fleeting state, very much like our thoughts and subsequent reactions to feeling overwhelmed. Similarly, it is useful for middle leaders to think about their inner ostrich as a temporary disposition. We can be overwhelmed when change occurs, and this can lead to high levels of stress. This is to be expected as we gradually orientate ourselves to change and workload challenges that rattle our beliefs and values. The key to ensuring the ostrich doesn't hamper our efforts to lead is by embracing this notion of rolling with it through broadening our frame of reference. Through elevated levels of self-awareness, the impact of ongoing change and our roles in that change can become less daunting.

As you read this chapter, after a recollection of my own experience with one particular "impossible" student, I will discuss the ostrich's common pain points and then provide six further self-awareness levers for overcoming those pain points. By learning to alleviate the negative energy of feeling overwhelmed, you will likely find your motivation levels rise. In turn you will cope better, develop greater resilience, and increase your capacity to roll with it rather than drown in it.

The Impossible Student

Mark is one student I will remember for the rest of my days. A colleague once described him as the student who was put on this planet for one purpose: to torment us all. (Know any of those?) I was generally successful with students who were somewhat behaviorally challenging or came from personal circumstances that made providing a truly equitable education very difficult. That may have been because, as a student, I also struggled with the whole experience of schooling. I understood their frustrations and difficulties in "doing" school. I taught Mark for two years, and over time, he gradually wore me down. I was still in the early years of my teaching career and had just started my work as a middle leader, taking on the role of physical education and health coordinator at the school.

This role meant more time out of the classroom as I dealt with increased administration demands and leading a team responsible for the provision, monitoring, and evaluation of our department curriculum, among many other things. However, my classroom responsibilities stayed the same. Then there was my teaching job! Part of my week would often include dodging chairs being thrown at me and dealing with outright refusals from Mark to do anything. That's when I wasn't restraining him from harming himself or others or repairing relationships with the rest of the class to maintain a learning culture. Time was also consumed encouraging my colleagues to take collective responsibility in our approach to Mark, because while he was in *my* class, he was *our* student.

Then one afternoon, nearly two years into my leadership role, my world came crashing down. I suffered from a professional meltdown. I had nothing left. I was suffering badly from compassion fatigue and struggling to manage my own expectations for my new leadership role. I wasn't coping and was avoiding many of the sources of my stress, including my role's core responsibilities.

Sitting in the conference room with my principal one bitterly cold winter afternoon, I felt like the seams were splitting on my promising career. The ostrich in me was becoming more and more prevalent, and I didn't want to raise my head from the sand for fear of what was to come. I was done. I had no reserves left, and there was nowhere to go. I was upset because I wasn't sure what else I could do for this student whose behavior was becoming increasingly unbearable. I had tried to save him, and, in the process, I had lost myself.

I will never forget my principal's words nor their intent:

> Gavin, you'll be no good to anybody, let alone yourself, if you don't focus on what you're in control of. You have expended energy on aspects of the job which you have no power over or can make decisions for. You have become overwhelmed by the things you aren't attending to, rather than those you are. You're the only person who is ultimately in control of yourself—no matter what you might otherwise say to yourself. You've let external factors override the internal resources you need to teach and lead, both now and into the future.

He then sent me home and gave me the following day off. Before I left, he added:

> I want some evidence that you've done some reflecting and reading on self-management. When you come back, we will chat about some ways forward for you and what you are becoming more self-aware of so that we can work on your capacity to cope with the job.

Through the power of self-reflection and with support from a benevolent boss, I began to understand the symbiotic relationship between self-management and management of others. Giving to others without first giving to ourselves is a sure road to compassion fatigue and burnout. Without stepping outside of myself, observing what was happening, and making meaningful adjustments to my approach at work, I very much doubt I would be still working in education, let alone helping other leaders.

The Ostrich's Pain Points

As we've discussed, being overwhelmed by change and the increased amounts of effort required of middle leaders can lead to avoidance. There is a significant link between this and what is known as avoidance coping in the field of psychology. So, what is avoidance coping, and what are the implications?

Avoidance coping is associated with discomfort and depression because it involves cognitive and behavioral attempts aimed at rejecting, diminishing, or otherwise avoiding dealing directly with unpleasant demands (Cronkite & Moos, 1995; Penley, Tomaka, & Wiebe, 2002). Also referred to as *escape coping*, avoidance coping is a type of maladaptive (not adjusting adequately to a situation or environment) coping whereby someone modifies their conduct to evade thinking, feeling, or doing things that cause them anguish (American Psychological Association, n.d.a).

Looking at the situation I described at the start of this chapter with the benefit of hindsight, it is obvious there were many things I was avoiding that ultimately led to my downfall. Most of these things were associated with myself, such as neglecting my health (including my eating, sleeping, and exercise patterns). My diminished capacity for coping with both my teaching and leadership responsibilities was a direct result of feeling sluggish because of how I was—or wasn't, really—looking after myself. Another stressor I was avoiding was finding ways to lead colleagues who I perceived as having more expertise because of their greater experience in the profession (and my relative younger age). Rather than share those thoughts or seek support and ideas, I buried them until their weight contributed to bringing me down. There were others, but these two were significant in bringing out the ostrich in me. As Maria T. M. Dijkstra and Astrid C. Homan (2016) remind us, any effort to avoid coping with the stressors involved with our roles can often exacerbate it. This can occur because circumventing things that are causing the stress can add to a feeling of being out of control. Subsequently, rather than avoiding stress, my avoidance brought about higher levels of distress.

My experience provided me with an opportunity to grow. Through building my awareness of the thoughts, emotions, and actions that drove me to this place of professional meltdown, I began to understand that stress can only be reduced by dealing with its source and seeking support from trusted colleagues and other professionals. I discovered sustainable ways to manage my stressors as opposed to avoiding them, some of which we will explore in this chapter.

Rather than bury our heads in the sand, we can learn to use another of the ostrich's unique abilities—the ability to observe vast distances. With the largest eyeball of any bird, ostriches can see more than two miles away (Aruba Ostrich Farm, n.d.). (If you remember nothing else from the book, this is something you can drop in at a dinner party.) By understanding the pain points that make us put our heads in the sand, we can elevate our self-awareness and embrace our inner ostrich's super-vision to take beneficial action.

Here are four common pain points to look out for: lack of focus, lack of motivation, complaining, and feeling out of depth.

Do I Lack Focus?

If you feel your ability to focus on the core responsibilities of your role has slipped, this may indicate you are avoiding stressors associated with your leadership. Lack of focus is a prevailing pain point for many of the leaders I coach and work with. In its simplest form, *focus* refers to our capacity to give particular attention to something (focused attention). This differs from *sustained attention*, where we can focus over a long period of time (or *stimuli attention*, where we can attend to something specific even when distractions surround us). Stress, however, can impede our cognition, attention, and memory (Harvard Health Publishing, 2021). The capacity to focus on anything may therefore be significantly impaired through the avoidance of those stressors causing us pain.

How many times have you found yourself talking with a colleague, only to walk away not having heard anything they said? While this can be a normal way of coping with the vast array of stimuli our brains have to contend with daily, it can also spill over into dangerous levels of inattention, leading to underperformance.

In the months and weeks leading up to my enforced leave, I remember feeling overwhelmed by my inability to sustain focus on one thing (far from ideal in the frenetic world of teaching). I was also procrastinating more than usual, finding ways to avoid aspects of my work I would typically embrace. This was evident in my avoidance of certain staff members who I felt were contributing to feelings of self-doubt—and the avoidance of any work associated with them. Instead, I would seek out activities that were unrelated to the things I should have been doing, such as preparing meeting agendas, filling in individual learning plans for Mark, and following up on the administrative tasks that came from our collaborative time. It was far easier to spend time organizing the staff get-together on a Friday night.

Over time, this lack of focus contributed to both my levels of distress and the feeling that I was accomplishing less, even if it wasn't the reality. If you notice your own focus decreasing, it may be an indication that the ostrich inside is spreading its feathers. It would pay to become conscious of why this is so you can align your focus with the things that matter most.

Do I Lack Motivation?

Lacking motivation and feeling disengaged from work can be a worrisome experience. In my coaching practice, as my clients become more aware of the stressors they have been avoiding, they often discover they have been suppressing a clash in their values and beliefs with those of their schools or colleagues. If they're not careful, this pain point can cause leaders to spiral deeper into feeling disenchanted about their chosen career, especially when coupled with an unsupportive or under-resourced school culture.

This combination can have middle leaders questioning their career choice as self-doubt and lack of perceived control take hold. Add to this a propensity to view others through a more negative lens, and they can experience decreasing levels of motivation as their focus moves further from the reasons they went into education in the first place.

I have witnessed some of my colleagues lose belief in their colleagues, teams, and school leadership. While my own faith in leadership was affirmed through the approach my principal took with me in my moment of disillusionment, my fear of failing my students—and by extension, their families—was real. My inner stories, revolving around what I thought I lacked rather than what was mine to gain in working with more experienced colleagues, had me questioning my leadership. This had a negative impact on my motivation to ultimately make a difference in people's lives.

Facing the underlying reasons for the stressors that contribute to a decreased level of motivation is critical to the growth of leaders. This is the opportunity to be found in the pain point. Upon my return to school, I felt more in control than at any time previously, and this reconnected me to my intrinsic motivations for working in education. It also provided me with a greater sense of empowerment—the power and authority to make decisions for myself that would contribute to greater opportunities, even when the inevitable difficulties of working in education hit.

Am I Complaining a Lot?

A pain point that is, in my experience, little spoken about is the amount of complaining we do. Excessive complaining to almost anyone who will listen (helping us justify our view of the world) is damaging on more than one front. It can contaminate an organization's culture, adding to workplace toxicity. It can also enable griping to take precedence over problem solving—a critical aspect for high-performing teams in particular. If you agree that culture can be defined by what is happening when no one is looking, then this becomes paramount.

Relationships that are built on mutual bursts of petulant moaning encourage the ostrich. It becomes easier to grumble about what is not working for you than to explore the causal reasons for why the stress exists in the first place. It is imperative that middle leaders grow their self-awareness to check in on how much complaining they may be doing and with whom. Given the precarious positions of middle leaders within schools and the potential impact they can have on all levels of the organization, this can become a growth point. If we are in a leadership position to help things be better, then we have an obligation to minimize our own levels of complaining. This can often indicate how effective middle leaders navigate the space between as they move from teacher to teacher leader.

Often middle leaders struggle to commit to complaining less because it has previously been an important ingredient in their relationships with fellow teachers. However, when they become middle leaders, the dynamics change, and they are in no position to complain—they would be like the spinning wheels of a car stuck in the mud. Instead, they need to join the ranks of leaders looking for ways to get the car (and its driver) safely out of the mud. That's a very different space to occupy for middle leaders. Having moved up in the hierarchy, their responsibility to evolving the culture of their organization increases. This can lead to a hard question:

> *Is the organization's mission more important than my relationship with this person—one that is based on a mutual disdain for all things that are wrong about the organization?*

Though I feel strongly that we condone the professional behaviors we walk past, when we stop and contribute to those negative behaviors, we give them even more oxygen. In my PLC work, I use the 10/90 rule, which I first came across working with Austin Buffum, a leading expert and author in the broad field of PLCs. The *10/90 rule* is essentially a lighthearted way of asking teams to consider whether they are spending 90 percent of their time admiring a problem and 10 percent finding solutions, or 10 percent of their time admiring the problem and 90 percent finding solutions (Rowe, 2021). This rule could be useful as you consider whether that pesky ostrich is at play. Is it blocking you from seeking the opportunities that digging deeper into your sources of stress might bring?

Do I Feel Out of My Depth?

Feeling out of depth is closely related to overwhelm. It can be recognized by our physiological reactions—if we are self-aware enough to notice them—to events and stimuli. It can indicate that we are far from growing; in fact, we are drowning. In this situation, *distress* (extreme sorrow, pain, or anxiety) takes over slowly from healthy levels of *eustress* (positive stress), which in contrast can be beneficial to health, performance, motivation, and emotional well-being. This potential pain point for leaders is most dangerous when self-awareness levels are low and a feeling of being out of control takes over, leading to a diminished capacity for self-management.

This is very much what happened to me in the scenario I shared at the start of this chapter. It wasn't sudden, even though it may have looked that way from the outside. It was stress compounding over time through a lack of insight and willingness to confront the realities of my situation, both as a teacher and as a middle leader.

These higher levels of distress manifested in overthinking and navel-gazing as my emotional wheels kept spinning—keeping me in the mud. This led to reduced joy in my work as the weight of responsibility combined with self-doubt.

The ostrich within each of us becomes a survival mechanism (as was the case with me), but unfortunately, it is more likely to contribute to our demise. Of all the pain points described in this chapter, feeling out of my depth was the hardest for me to move away from and see any possibility of growth in. Distress does that to all of us. Prolonged distress contributes to an even worse prognosis and can even produce physical effects. Research is conclusive: "Many disorders originate from stress, especially if the stress is severe and prolonged" (Yaribeygi, Panahi, Sahraei, Johnston, & Sahebkar, 2017, p. 1066).

The following self-awareness levers and associated tips help minimize any chance that distress becomes a prolonged part of your leadership. These levers will also help you gain focus, increase your motivation, and have more productive conversations rather than resorting to endless complaining.

Self-Awareness Levers to Overcome the Ostrich's Pain Points

As I set out the levers that will help you overcome and grow from the pain points I have described, I will also share how they played out for me. I'll also give you the chance to use these levers on a problem or challenge that, in true ostrich style, you may have been avoiding.

The six levers are as follows.

1. Dig in.
2. Break it down.
3. Seek support.
4. Enlarge your frame of reference.
5. Accept that change is personal and inevitable.
6. Lighten up to lighten loads.

These levers have value in potentially enabling your self-awareness. They can help you develop habits that move you from thinking of them as potentially good ideas to genuinely incorporating them into how you work. They encourage us to focus on how we think about the pace of change and the complexities of our work, ultimately helping reduce overwhelm.

As you read, I encourage you to pay attention to the levers you feel most connected to and explore for yourself the positive implications of focusing on those levers. What benefits could they possibly bring you?

Stoic philosopher Marcus Aurelius (2006) writes, "If you are distressed by anything external, the pain is not due to the thing itself, but to your estimate of it; and this you have the power to revoke at any moment" (p. 64). The idea is that our thoughts and beliefs about a situation, rather than the situation itself, are what cause us to feel overwhelmed or distressed. As the following six levers will illustrate, by recognizing our power to control our thoughts and beliefs, we can gain greater control over our emotional responses to difficult situations.

1. Dig In

The first lever is about neutralizing, using two major strategies, the anxieties that get in the way of our work. This hinges first on understanding and prioritizing our values ahead of our fears, recognizing that we may feel a certain way when these values are compromised or challenged. It then moves to having us consider the assumptions we may be basing these fears on and challenging them in ways that can help us.

Put Values Before Fears

In my role as a teacher and subsequent leader, I had very high expectations of myself because I valued accomplishment and achievement so much. This came from a deep but flawed belief that I needed external validation to feel satisfied. While achievement and accomplishment are still important to me, over time, I have learned to value myself first in my ultimate pursuit to support others to grow. This helped to alleviate the fear of failure I once held on to.

It is our capacity for morality that separates human beings from other animals (Ayala, 2010). As individuals, the values we hold dear shape our morals and also our societies. *Values* are those beliefs we place great importance on.

Examining your situation, what values are being compromised or challenged in ways that are creating anxiety for you? Consider the following examples of values when addressing this question.

- Acceptance
- Accountability
- Autonomy
- Balance
- Change
- Clarity
- Compassion

- Courage
- Decisiveness
- Efficiency
- Fairness
- Gratitude
- Honesty
- Hope

- Independence
- Influence
- Integrity
- Joy or fun
- Justice
- Kindness
- Knowledge

- Loyalty
- Openness
- Optimism
- Promise-keeping
- Respect
- Selflessness
- Sincerity
- Success
- Wisdom

Challenge Assumptions

An *assumption* is something you believe to be true without proof. One assumption that was a real stumbling block for me was that I could be, and needed to be, all things to all people I worked with. This was rooted in my need to be needed and was shaped by the identity I had formed around what I felt it meant to be a teacher and a leader. This created a lot of tension for me and ultimately shaped the direction of my work with educators in helping them become more collaborative in their approaches to their work. I have since come to believe that I can't be all things to all people unless I am that to myself first. I now work with countless educators to guide them in empowering themselves in their own lives while they strive to do the same for others.

Examining your situation, what assumptions are you making that are creating anxiety for you?

2. Break It Down

Breaking things down is an important process because it enables us to feel more in control, which can reduce the anxiety associated with feeling out of control. It also assists in making tasks feel manageable and helps support our belief that we are both capable and competent. Thinking in terms of doing one thing at a time, in combination with making realistic lists (more detail on this shortly), can be useful.

Do One Thing at a Time

Upon my return to work, it was important that I maintained a sense of control over the sources of my stress, including teaching Mark and leading my team. I wrote down four things that seemed reasonable and realistic.

1. Put Mark on a behavior plan and seek the well-being team's support.
2. Ask my boss for advice about meetings and working with my colleagues.
3. Go to bed earlier and at the same time each night (and research different ways to fall asleep).
4. Manage my expectations through sharing my concerns and ideas with my team-teaching partner and trusted colleague, and seek permission to check in with her when I needed to. I knew she would say yes but would respect her choice to say no.

The outcomes of committing to these specific actions were valuable. I felt a greater level of support, a lessening of self-imposed pressure, and a real increase in efficacy and clarity in my work as a teacher and a leader. It was a gradual process, of course; forming new habits always is.

What chunks might you break down your challenge into to make it more manageable?

Write a List

I committed to a weekly list of priorities rather than a daily one, which had been creating feelings of overwhelm for me. This worked well and broke down my thoughts and responsibilities into manageable and realistic pieces. I used Eisenhower's priority matrix (MindTools, n.d.) to organize my priorities into four categories.

1. Important and urgent
2. Not urgent but important
3. Not important but urgent
4. Not important or urgent

I reviewed my list every Friday afternoon before going home and reordered these priorities based on where I had gotten to that week. This started a process that helped me make peace with incompletion. I also (except where I couldn't) added estimations for when things should be completed rather than deadlines. It helped to keep the ostrich at bay and continues to be effective to this day.

How might this manifest as a weekly or daily list to support you to stay on track and remain self-aware?

3. Seek Support

Ways to seek support include regulating and delegating and finding an empathetic ear.

Regulate and Delegate

Regulating is the process of applying new habits through elevating our awareness of the thoughts and actions we most need to attend to. It can be aided by enabling others to assist us.

It was important for me that I shared my struggles wholeheartedly with my boss and teaching partner. I shared my priorities (and lists) with them to feel less alone in my thoughts. This also helped me remain aware of my thinking, emotions, and actions as I went about growing from my experiences. Their informal but unwavering support helped me regulate my new ways of working as I learned over time to react less like an ostrich.

I also sought out more opinions, advice, and work from team members who were more experienced than I was. This form of delegation had the unintended outcome of leaving them feeling more ownership over our work and more connection to me as their leader. It was just a more respectful way of working and proved to be the start of my lifelong journey to develop as a coach.

Who might support you to regulate new habits that will allow you to overcome your challenge, and what can you ask others to do to help you?

Find an Empathetic Ear (Beware the Complaining Cycle)

Locating a colleague or friend who is genuinely empathetic is both valuable and not an easy task. Empathy differs from sympathy because it comes from a place of acceptance and understanding rather than pity and the need to save. The combination of nonjudgment and unwavering acceptance of where you are can be extremely valuable in assisting you to overcome challenges associated with the ostrich.

Anyone who has these qualities in spades is a gift. They truly attempt to swim around in our world to understand what might be going on, suspending judgment without making it about them. They don't necessarily tell you what you want to hear, but you cannot question that their intention is to support you in whatever it is you are seeking. I was lucky enough to have that in a family member and a colleague. I sought them out each time I felt the inner ostrich emerge, if for no other reason than to ensure I confronted what I was feeling rather than avoiding it.

Whom might be someone you can turn to who truly listens with the intention to understand without making it about them?

4. Enlarge Your Frame of Reference

I have always read to challenge my thinking and to grow. During this phase of my middle leadership journey, I read William Bridges's (2004) book *Transitions: Making Sense of Life's Changes*. It helped me enormously in enlarging my frame of reference and moving out of the professional bubble in which I resided. Bridges (2004) helped me see that what I was experiencing was a normal part of any transition period. I embraced the notion that change represents a shift in the external situation (which for me was the end of being solely a classroom teacher as my responsibilities increased), into the transition stage, which centers more on psychological reorientation in response to change. He refers to this transition as the *neutral zone* (Bridges, 2004).

How long we spend in the neutral zone depends on many factors, but it always takes time. This enlarging of my frame of reference was reassuring, humbling, and a relief. It helped me transition into a space where I could begin to accept and embrace my responsibilities as a middle leader. I still use this frame, which has branched out into other learnings, assisting me to use my self-awareness to monitor how I am navigating ongoing change in my personal and professional life and the impact that has on others.

What might assist you in taking a bird's-eye view of the situation? What might you notice as a result?

5. Accept That Change Is Personal and Inevitable

Leading my first team and being part of an executive broadened my perspective. One of my first realizations was the importance of checking in with the people who are directly impacted by any change we may lead. This was missing from my earlier clumsy attempts at establishing credibility by demonstrating what I knew rather than what they did. It was a very unconscious way of leading. After I returned from my leave, I began over time to observe people's responses to change as well as their concerns. Rather than reject them or become frustrated, I used these occasions as opportunities to inquire further.

I learned that any change process will have all of us (more or less) go through three stages: (1) a self-centered stage of asking how the change will affect us; followed by (2) a more task-orientated stage of asking what we might have to do and what it affects in our job; lastly (if we get there) we (3) start asking ourselves about the impact the change is having and whether there might be other ways of getting even better results (Hall & Hord, 2011; Southwest Educational Development Laboratory, n.d.). These stages, derived from the Concerns-Based Adoption Model, heightened my awareness of how I and others experience the change process and work out the best ways of trying to meet everyone's needs. I learned that sometimes all people need is to know you are trying. After all, it's people who implement change—and it's middle leaders who are the linchpin to many of the change initiatives in schools.

What change are you currently supporting or leading in which it may pay to check in with all who might be affected? How might this information tell you what they will need from you?

6. Lighten Up to Lighten the Load

Not to diminish the importance of the work we do as educators, but humor can be a great antidote to the lack of joy the ostrich sometimes leads us to. I have valued humor and laughter for as long as I can remember. Both in my classroom and beyond I have always found it important to not take myself too seriously (but to still take the work seriously). After all, the longer a life becomes, the shorter it gets—so it is important we find joy in it.

As I reflected on the pivotal moment in my career that I described at the start of this chapter, I realized how joyless my work was becoming, even though I had loved teaching from the moment I first stepped into a classroom as an undergraduate. This was very disconcerting. To return to that place of joy, there were six actions I applied (over time) and continue to apply today.

1. See the humor in something I find difficult—like writing a book!
2. Write down something I am grateful for at least once per week in my "busy working on myself" journal.
3. Pause to occasionally ask myself, "What is the worst thing that could happen here?" (And work backward from there.)
4. Embrace people who make me feel good and who I can laugh with.
5. Engage my senses by being present and in the moment. This is a work in progress.
6. Remember our life is temporary. I was born in 1971 and am living my days without knowledge of what my closing date will be. 1971–? What is sometimes referred to as *death awareness* helps me live in the present moment more enjoyably, even when that moment may be a tough one.

If your predicament was a comedy show on Netflix, what might be some of the things you could have a hearty laugh over?

When we learn to overcome overwhelm and develop habits that make it less likely that our inner ostrich will appear, the result is a greater sense of control and increasing levels of competence and confidence in our capacity to lead. We find change less daunting and are more likely to look for the benefits as we transition from what we once did to what might be emerging ahead of us. As outlined in the beginning of this chapter, this doesn't mean we ignore the reasons we feel overwhelmed. In truth, we seek them out, stare them down, and leave them behind in pursuit of new patterns of thinking and doing—patterns that help us navigate the inevitable changes associated with leadership and enable us to assist others to do the same.

Emerge Exercises: The Self-Work

Let's dig deeper into the pain points associated with being the ostrich. Use these stems to capture what's emerged for you as you have read this chapter and what you might do with that knowledge.

- As a result of reading this chapter, I think it's important to . . .
- I believe this will help me to . . .
- It will help me to think . . .
- It will help me to feel . . .
- It will help me to do . . .
- I will be more aware of my physiological reactions by . . .
- I will consider developing in my personality a capacity to . . .
- I am more motivated to . . .
- I will ask others to take notice of my commitment to . . .

> **emerge**
>
> What's the most valuable insight that is emerging for you from this chapter? How might that insight help you move forward?

In the depths of winter, I finally learned that within me there lay an invincible summer.

—Albert Camus

CHAPTER 7

The Imposter: Overcoming Self-Limiting Beliefs

You'll learn to begin
To trust the voice within

—Christina Aguilera & Glen Ballard

As you reflect on your leadership, what do you notice in the quiet recesses of your mind? Do you even think of yourself as a leader? Do you acknowledge your accomplishments and what brought you to this point? Do you believe that your colleagues, students, school, and community are better off because, at least in part, of what you do?

These are important questions from the perspective of illuminating any potential self-limiting beliefs you might hold. As discussed in chapter 4 (page 45), our thoughts can lead us to feelings of inadequacy that contribute to us feeling like fakes, like we don't belong in the spaces we occupy. The voice within is certainly a powerful one and has the potential to either restrict our impact or increase it.

In biology, a colony of organisms can limit its own growth by its behaviors. Once it reaches a particular number, it may begin to emit waste that is ultimately poisonous to the colony. In certain circumstances, as is the case with parasites, the self-limiting characteristic of a colony may be favorable to the colony's continuous survival. But in the case of our leadership identities, self-limiting beliefs are more likely to result in our professional demise than in our survival.

Our self-limiting beliefs can lead us to view ourselves as imposters—shaking our confidence, diluting our purpose, reducing our capacity to elicit genuine change, and constraining our ability to exert real influence. Even when our beliefs aren't serving us well, we tend to hold on to them. This is what makes them limiting. They reduce our capacity to flourish in our roles and assist others to do the same.

Some refer to this as *imposter syndrome* (also known as *imposter phenomenon, fraud syndrome, perceived fraudulence,* or *imposter experience*). This term describes high-achieving individuals who, despite their objective successes, fail to internalize their accomplishments and have persistent self-doubt and fear of being exposed as a fraud or imposter (Kolligian & Sternberg, 1991).

This fear drives our thoughts. However, like any thought you may have over the course of the day, that doesn't mean it is real. It is just a thought, and your reality comes from how you process that thought. I might be sitting here writing this chapter and thinking it won't be helpful enough. But this is not real; it's just a thought. Ultimately, the reality of how helpful this is rests with you.

So, I have a choice. I can believe the self-limiting thought I just had and stop writing. I could procrastinate further and decide to do more research and miss my deadline. I could give up the writing process altogether, tell myself I'm just not a writer, and let the imposter take complete hold of my thoughts, feelings, and subsequent actions. Alternatively, I can acknowledge the thought, stare it down, and tell it in no uncertain terms (I'll keep it nice) to go away because it's not real.

Moments like these are littered through our days, weeks, and months. They play out in different ways, and if we're not careful, they can grow the imposter archetype within us to unhealthy levels. For me and many of the colleagues I have coached, this is a real risk.

In this chapter, I will share with you the power of how two words assisted me to overcome self-limiting beliefs before then helping you discover five self-awareness levers to combat the pain points related to feeling like an imposter.

The Voice Within

By shifting the stories you tell yourself and visualizing a more compelling way forward, the voice within will quiet your inner imposter. Your self-assurance will emerge and quell any self-doubt that may exist as your voice within becomes more friend than foe. As you'll see in coming pages, the language we choose to use in how we think has a big bearing on how we relate to ourselves. As writer Julie Beck (2016) puts it, "Language is the hallmark of humanity—it allows us to form deep relationships and complex societies. But we also use it when we're all alone; it shapes even our silent relationships with ourselves."

Two Words

If I am to be honest with myself and with you, I would say that overcoming the imposter archetype has been the most professionally challenging aspect of my leadership development. The self-limiting beliefs associated with this archetype can be paralyzing. On the other hand, it has also provided me with the greatest opportunities for growth, both in my identity as a leader and as a person.

The imposter is the ego running wild. It's easy not to think of the imposter as our egos because we tend to connect the ego with overconfidence, not underconfidence. But when we think of ego as just a sense of self (neither positive nor negative), then we can see that the imposter archetype has us anchor ourselves in self-perpetuating thoughts, crippling our capacity to truly lead learning in others.

I knew I was genuinely engaged in a process of freeing myself from the imposter (and my ego) when I no longer felt the need to entertain thoughts such as the following.

- "I'm not smart enough to write this book."
- "I'm too young to be a leader in this school."
- "I'm not brilliant enough to deliver this keynote."
- "I don't have enough experience to create this program."
- "I'm out of my depth in dealing with these colleagues who are more experienced than me."
- "I don't know enough to be in this position."
- "I'm not sure I can be who this person needs me to be."

This is not an exhaustive list, and since my early days, I have been gripped to some degree by the imposter. I know it formed early in my life, as these habitual patterns of thinking about ourselves often do. I mentioned at the start of this book that I wasn't always a great student and that I have struggled with feeling adequate as a learner right from the beginning of school. This self-doubt subsequently flowed through to my identity as a teacher and leader. When I've shared such thoughts with my colleagues, they are usually surprised because I disguise this self-doubt by acting confidently—sometimes overconfidently! At times, I've even looked for deficits in others to provide myself with some deluded sense of status.

These beliefs, developed over the course of my lifetime, became my way of protecting myself from pain. This pain was born out of fear—a fear of being seen and heard. It feels bizarre to even write that. Here I am: an author, public speaker, coach, and educator who has, over many years, developed a fear of being seen and heard. I certainly could have chosen a more suitable career path!

These self-limiting beliefs started at a young age and evolved throughout my lived experiences. They hampered many opportunities for forming new beliefs that were more conducive to my own social, emotional, and cognitive growth. And these beliefs came from a cumulative process of feeling unworthy and invalidated. There are many reasons for this that I now understand (and which could fill another book). But what's most important to take from this is that our self-limiting beliefs are an attempt to protect us from pain, both now and in the future.

So how did I end up here: a quietly confident, self-aware, and self-accepting leader? Let me say first that we are all works in progress. A more helpful way of thinking about overcoming these challenges might be imagining a series of hurdles that we leap over each time. The further we travel and must jump, the lower the hurdles seem until we are running with fewer and fewer hurdles in sight.

For me, the pivotal moment came just before I was to deliver a keynote on the power of PLCs before 250 of my peers. A dear colleague of mine noticed my nerves, sensing my fear as the clock counted down. My mind was lost in a sea of thoughts, all pertaining to what could go wrong and why I was doing it (the ego was strong that morning). In her own quiet and reassuring way, my colleague gently grabbed my left hand (I remember that because my presentation clicker was occupying my nervous right hand) and said two words that completely overcame my self-doubt: "You're enough!" With that, she smiled reassuringly and walked off to take her seat in the audience. It's hard to describe what those two words did for me that morning and ever since, but I walked onto the stage calm, present, and ready—and I gave what I consider to be the best keynote I have ever delivered. I was simply being myself, and trusting what I know, what I offer, and how I offer it. And that was enough, on that day and into the future.

That moment in time propelled me forward and quieted some of the self-limiting beliefs that had plagued me many times in my leadership journey. Those two words didn't center on external validation but on internal validation. They said that in that moment, I was enough and everything I had was all I needed. And that's all that mattered.

That morning, something shifted for me in my self-awareness, and I began working earnestly to focus my awareness on a place of internal validation. This reduced my need for external validation because I understood, for the first time, wherever I was at any moment, regardless of where I was going, I was enough.

But as we all know, understanding something and applying it are two different things. Over the next few pages, I want to share with you what I've learned from my own experience and from the privilege of supporting my colleagues to quiet the imposter within.

The Imposter's Pain Points

As mentioned at the start of this chapter, thoughts are temporary. They come and go each moment, and yet they tell us a story that we believe to be true. These thoughts become the language of our lives, and we hold them dear as though they were absolute truth, when in reality, they are just thoughts. They shape the way we approach things and are critical in revealing to us the self-limiting beliefs that may not be serving us well.

Returning to Beck's (2016) understanding that language "shapes even our silent relationships with ourselves," these silent self-relationships are born from more than six thousand thoughts every day, according to a study by Julie Tseng and Jordan Poppenk (2020) published in *Nature Communications*. That means there is ample opportunity for self-limiting beliefs to take hold and develop because our beliefs are simply what we consider to be true based on the thoughts that we have.

In the same paper, the researchers devised a way of isolating what they call *thought worms*, defined as sequential moments when we focus on the same idea. That moniker is quite apt given our topic (Tseng & Poppenk, 2020). Self-limiting beliefs in the form of a thought worm can burrow in and embed themselves so deeply into our unconsciousness over time that we no longer recognize them, and we therefore accept them as true. Our unconsciousness is rich soil for thought worms, which limit our potential to see the possibilities that arise from examining and challenging these thoughts.

If we are not careful, these unhelpful thought worms can take hold so strongly that we mistake them for reality. The fact of the matter is, however, that they are simply thoughts. We can choose to not be defined by them or, at the very least, examine them with the intent to challenge their premise. Failing to do so can affect us in real and adverse ways, including the following.

- Fueling a negative state of mind, impeding us from embracing new possibilities and life experiences while also harming our emotional well-being
- Clinging to preconceived notions about others that can hinder our ability to interact fruitfully, eventually affecting the caliber of our output
- Prioritizing safety over the need to challenge our self-limiting beliefs and their associated thoughts to the detriment of genuine empowerment for both ourselves and others

- Keeping us from enjoying the lives we want to live through performing as a version of ourselves rather than being ourselves
- Suffocating the possibility for growth and development
- Perpetuating a version of self that we feel others expect from us but that deep down we don't want for ourselves, leading to a disconnect in living authentically

These pain points are real for many middle leaders in their quest to learn about who they are and who they can become as leadership beckons. According to Amy Morin (2014), unhealthy beliefs (from which these pain points grow) can be classified in three ways.

1. Beliefs about self
2. Beliefs about others
3. Beliefs about the world

These are a useful frame with which to think about how what we believe to be true could be holding us back. For example, *I am not a people person* (belief about self); *others don't understand me* (belief about others); and *there will never be world peace* (belief about the world). It takes courage and a willingness to confront the voice within to change the way we have come to see ourselves by challenging the very beliefs that have been holding us back. As Adam Grant (2021) argues, we don't have to believe or internalize everything we think or feel. This is an invitation to let go of beliefs that no longer serve you well and to value mental flexibility over stubborn consistency. Knowing what we don't know, in this sense, becomes wisdom.

Self-Awareness Levers to Overcome the Imposter's Pain Points

A variation on a famous quote by C. S. Lewis (2001) states:

> There is one thing, and only one in the whole universe which we know more about than that we could learn from external observation. That one thing is ourselves. We have, so to speak, inside information, we are in the know. (pp. 23–24)

So, what are you in the know about that could help you dispense with that pesky imposter when they show up? And when you become more aware of what you find, what do you do next? Let's take a deeper dive into five levers for elevating your self-awareness so that you can confront the imposter and overcome its grip on you.

The five levers in this chapter will raise your consciousness to envision possibilities you didn't know or feel existed before. They will help you to de–thought worm your self-limiting beliefs and escape from the clutches of your unconsciousness to find a more helpful inner voice. These five levers are as follows.

1. Pause and identify the self-limiting belief.
2. Understand your self-story.
3. Explore the what-ifs.
4. Paint a mental picture.
5. Make some decisions.

These levers help us recognize our own self-limiting beliefs when they surface, use that recognition to reframe how we think about those beliefs, and challenge their very existence. They represent opportunities to engage in what is often referred to in the field of psychology as *cognitive restructuring*. Once we embed these levers more consciously into our ways of being, we can use them with—and for—others, increasing our influence and impact as middle leaders.

1. Pause and Identify the Self-Limiting Belief

Judith Beck (2005, 2011) suggests there are three main categories of negative core beliefs about the self from her research.

1. Helplessness
2. Unlovability
3. Worthlessness

When the pandemic hit at the beginning of 2020, the two words *I'm enough* just didn't seem enough anymore. I was forced (as many people were) to pause my career. My hometown of Melbourne, Australia, ended up becoming arguably the most locked down city in the world, and when this all started, it was terrifying for many of us. To some degree, I felt mentally paralyzed. Fear permeated every pore in my body. My physiological reaction to the sudden lockdown and immediate postponement of all my work resulted in constant headaches, lethargy, and a short fuse. At this early stage of the pandemic, the underpinning belief that limited my capacity to find a way forward centered around the first of Beck's (2005, 2011) core beliefs: helplessness. My competence was rattled; I felt vulnerable and out of my depth.

When my work conditions changed as a result of the pandemic, I felt deserted and experienced some cognitive paralysis. I lacked the ability to turn the situation into an opportunity simply because I lacked the belief that I could find a way when things seemed so bleak. However, I found that just pausing to identify for myself what I was feeling and examining the beliefs I held that contributed to these feelings was useful to me. It was one thing I could do when everything else seemed so out of control.

Using Socratic questioning can be helpful in identifying self-limiting beliefs, and it certainly was for me. At its foundation, Socratic questioning (named after the ancient Greek philosopher, Socrates) enables us to examine the validity of our ideas (Changing Works, n.d.). The questions that were most helpful to me, and that I often use with others, include these.

- Where is the evidence for the helplessness (or other emotion) I'm feeling?
- What assumptions am I making based on this situation?
- Are my beliefs based on an emotional reaction or on actual evidence in front of me?

Through journaling, talking, or even just pondering our thoughts in response to these questions, we can more effectively identify the self-limiting beliefs that might be holding us back. For me, it became clear that these fears, while totally valid and understandable, were based purely on emotion. They weren't and didn't have to become the reality of my future. So, where to next?

2. Understand Your Self-Story

By pausing and identifying some of the beliefs I was holding, I started to apply what I taught others in my coaching and relational intelligence work. I wrote down the self-stories that were playing out in my mind and looked for ways to edit them. These self-stories, born out of a belief that I was helpless to do anything, played out in different ways and spiraled out of control. This is sometimes referred to as *dirty anxiety* (LeJeune, 2007). Here's an example:

> *I am going to lose the majority of my work because my clients won't need what I offer anymore.*

This can quickly spiral into the following.

- We will suffer financially.
- I won't be able to provide the same opportunities for my family.
- I will not be as satisfied in my work.
- I am out of my depth.
- I am not needed.
- I need a drink!

As I examined this self-story, two things became clear to me. The first was that I was wasting energy thinking about what could happen in the future (but that hadn't happened) rather than what I could be doing right now to alleviate any risk (and worry) of it happening. The second was that accepting the situation and dealing with it in the present enabled me to take control in a moment when I felt so out of control. This was a breakthrough because it illuminated what was going on underneath and challenged my self-limiting belief that I was helpless in this circumstance.

One powerful way to do this (which I will ask you to try in the emerge exercises at the end of this chapter, page 97) is to write down how these self-stories might be expressed. These could start with any of the following stems.

- I believe . . .
- I think . . .
- I feel . . .
- I am fearful of . . .
- I am . . .
- I will . . .
- I won't . . .

Let me take one of the thoughts I mentioned just a little further to illustrate how this works. Behind the thought *I am not needed* is a deeper truth: *I am fearful of not being needed by my clients anymore because the pandemic has changed their needs*. Delving into and articulating a range of self-stories like these will support you to observe, examine, and work with a broader collection of thoughts using the levers I outline in this chapter.

3. Explore the What-Ifs

My self-stories were all born out of fear. I accepted this and understood it to be a perfectly natural response given the circumstances. Allowing myself to pause and accept how I was feeling and thinking provided the stepping stones to a different—and healthier—imagined future. In essence, I was freer in my mind to explore some possibilities rather than focusing on my negative predictions about what the sudden lockdown would bring me and those I love.

What-ifs are about embracing a way of thinking that focuses on what the possibilities might be if we were to consider a situation in a different light. The concept is an important part of the work I do with schools in challenging and supporting them to becoming more collaborative problem solvers in achieving their school-improvement goals. Picture a continuum that begins with *Yeah, but* . . . at the 0 end, and finishes at 10 with *What if?* At this point in my life, I would have ranked myself a 1 on the what-if scale—at most! To move me closer to a 10, I needed to ask myself two questions.

1. What might be some of the ways I could think to overcome these challenges?
2. In what ways could my self-story change or shift?

As I thought more deeply about these questions, three possibilities occurred.

1. Everything will change.
2. I'm out of my depth.
3. People will no longer need what I have to offer.

Though my natural inclination was to worry about these possibilities, I used what-if thinking to turn my fears into opportunities. Though I was concerned that things would change, I realized that things *always* change—that's just life! Accepting that fact meant I felt more balanced, calm, and able to regulate the strong emotions I was feeling. My decision to use what-if thinking helped me realize that I've been out of my depth before—and that's when I'd learned the most and made significant positive changes to my life. I started to see that people may need what I had to offer more than they had before, and that gave me energy.

As I applied what-if thinking to these questions and my initial responses, the following possibilities started to emerge.

- Everything will change.

  What-if thinking: "Things always change—that's life! (Acceptance)"

- I'm out of my depth.

  What-if thinking: "I have been out of my depth before. (That's when you learn.)"

- People will no longer need what I have to offer.

  What-if thinking: "People may need me more than ever. (They may just need me differently.)"

Articulating these what-ifs in our thinking is an important way to utilize our cognitive flexibility (adapting our behaviors and thoughts to new, changing, or unexpected events; CogniFit, n.d.). This assists us to relate empathetically to ourselves and our situation. For me, what-ifs helped me open my mind to imagine some possibilities; rather than constantly identifying the roadblock, I was able to envision a different, less scary future. Through committing to exploring the what-ifs, you develop your capacity for self-awareness and learn how to worry more wisely.

4. Paint a Mental Picture

Renowned empowerment expert and coach Jack Canfield (n.d.) names four powerful benefits that can be achieved by incorporating visualization techniques into our ways of thinking.

According to Canfield (n.d.), visualization techniques can do the following.

1. Activate the creative subconscious, which starts generating creative ideas to achieve our goals.
2. Program our brains to perceive and recognize the resources needed to achieve our goals.
3. Activate the law of attraction, drawing to us the people, resources, and circumstances we need.
4. Build the internal motivation to take the necessary actions for success.

When I began to use *visualization*, painting a mental picture, I started to feel a shift. I knew I was becoming more resourceful and letting go of some of the early fear that had gripped me. I started to picture opportunities and what I could do, given I could no longer travel and do my work in the ways—or with the people and organizations—that I had before. I started to outline what my what-if thinking could look, sound, and feel like if I were to embrace that thinking for real. I explored how my colleagues might need me differently and what opportunities might exist to create genuine solutions to challenges I had seen in my work over fifteen years but had never had the time to do anything about.

Ideas not accessible to me at the onset of the pandemic started to flow more freely. These included professional ideas such as writing a new book, developing a much-needed program, engaging in deeper research, and furthering my private coaching practice. I played these all out in my mind, visualizing the possibilities. I used the following three questions to ascertain how connected I felt to the ideas that came to me.

1. How would it look if I was successful?
2. What would it sound like if I was successful?
3. How would I feel about doing that?

See how this works for you by considering the following powerful questions to explore the self-stories and what-ifs of your own situation.

1. What would I see myself doing in relation to my what-ifs?
2. What would I hear myself saying in relation to my what-ifs?
3. How would I be feeling in relation to enacting my what-ifs?

I also drew on close and trusted colleagues (who wouldn't just tell me what they thought I should do) to support me in my thinking. This all helped me make decisions that transitioned me into the next two years of work as the pandemic took over how we all lived.

5. Make Some Decisions

I was both physiologically and psychologically ready to commit to some firm decisions. In the process of reaching this point, I had honored how I was feeling and accepted these emotions legitimately without harsh self-judgment. I checked in at the source and paused to understand the thoughts that contributed to these feelings. This gave me a chance to work on how I could think differently about them, leading me to potential alternatives.

I faced off with the imposter in me and won. The imposter initially had me question whether I was worthy, able, or even resilient enough to prevail through these difficult times, let alone prosper. I applied these helpful levers to grow my self-awareness and navigate uncertain and destabilizing events. This all helped me make some decisions, including committing to developing a program for educators that supported them to navigate their thinking. The program, drawing on my years of experience as a coach, helped these educators boost their professional impact and well-being. At the time of writing this book, that relational intelligence program has helped hundreds of educators—and that list is growing. Without using some of these key levers of self-awareness to overcome my own self-limiting beliefs, the program wouldn't be having any impact at all.

Now, turn your attention to you. How can you use learnings from this chapter to recognize any self-limiting beliefs? How will you leverage those beliefs to emerge in ways that help rather than hinder you as a leader? Given that our thoughts become our behaviors, which of your thoughts provide you with the opportunity to behave in ways beneficial to yourself and those you lead? Behavioral scientist and habits expert BJ Fogg (2019) explains that planting a good seed in a good spot compares to picking the right small behavior and sequencing it correctly because it can result in growth without the need for additional motivation. The seed will naturally flourish and blossom, just like the behavior will naturally become part of your routine.

To the good seed and spot we go.

Emerge Exercises: The Self-Work

Let's dig deeper into the pain points associated with being the imposter. Use these exercises to capture what's emerged for you as you have read this chapter and what you might do with that knowledge. I recommend you spend some time thinking about and committing your responses to the page. Come back to them whenever you feel you need to. When the time is right, perhaps share your thinking with someone you trust, someone who will provide their own perspective and support you in taking action.

Pause and Identify the Self-Limiting Belief

Name a difficulty or situation that you would like to overcome in your leadership.

As you examine your beliefs about this challenge, name any self-limiting beliefs and where they might come from. Once you've identified the self-limiting beliefs at play, respond to the following questions in your journal.

- Which of Beck's (2005, 2011) three categories of negative core beliefs about the self—(1) helplessness, (2) unlovability, and (3) worthlessness—do each of your self-limiting beliefs belong to?
- How does each belief make you feel?
- Where is the evidence for what you feel?
- What assumptions are you making based on this situation?
- Are your beliefs based more on emotional reaction or on factual evidence in front of you?

Understand Your Self-Story

Using quotation marks, write down at least four of the self-stories you engage in that stem from these beliefs and emotions. For example, "People will no longer need what I have to offer."

Explore the What-Ifs

How might you rewrite those self-stories in ways that could open you up to new possibilities? With this question in mind, rewrite each of those self-stories as what-ifs that construct a more compelling narrative. For example, the self-story I offered first could be rewritten, "People may need me more than ever. (They may just need me differently.)"

Paint a Mental Picture

In your journal, answer the following three questions about each rewritten self-story.

1. How might it look if I am successful in thinking this way?
2. How might it sound if I am successful in thinking this way?
3. How might I feel when I am successful in applying this thinking to my leadership?

Make Some Decisions

Now it's time to make some decisions. Complete the following stems in your journal.

- Some possible decisions I could make because of examining this thinking include . . .
- The decisions I'm most drawn to are . . .
- This is because . . .
- The support I can draw from to help me commit to these decisions are . . .
- As a result of taking myself through this process, I am feeling more . . .

> **emerge**
>
> As a result of exploring this chapter, what would you hope to see in yourself three years from now that doesn't seem evident in how you lead right now?

You have the power in the present moment to change limiting beliefs and consciously plant the seeds for the future of your choosing. As you change your mind, you change your experience.

—Serge Kahili King

CHAPTER 8

The Dynamo: Overcoming Not Having Enough Time

Slow down everyone
You're moving too fast

—Jack Johnson

Before you're tempted to stop reading and curse me ("This guy doesn't understand how busy I am and what's expected of me!"), please hang on! You've made it this far. I know you're busy and feeling pressed for time, but keep going. As mentioned at the start of this book, I believe many authors write about the very things they strive to incorporate into their own lives, and for me, slowing down is one of them. However, I'm pleased to report I'm having more wins than losses these days in my battle to overcome that feeling of dread associated with limited time.

The fact is middle leaders are constantly juggling growing responsibilities—and the desire to have an impact—while also trying to lead satisfying personal lives. As mentioned in chapter 4 (page 45), overcoming issues relating to a lack of time is one of the greatest frustrations of middle leaders. As Wenner and Campbell (2017) point out:

> When we examined the literature to identify those factors that inhibited the effectiveness of teacher leadership, we noted themes that align with the adverse effects of teacher leadership on teacher leaders. Particularly, lack of time seems reasonably connected with the stresses and difficulties teacher leaders reported in these roles. (p. 162)

No one has a monopoly on the perils of squeezing as much into twenty-four hours as they can to try to exert their influence. It sometimes amazes me that in less collaborative school cultures, we can live in parallel universes, thinking no one could possibly understand how hard we work in the little time we have. But when we afford ourselves the chance to look outside the bubble, we can see busyness everywhere. We can also see the effects of this busyness, including a decreased ability to focus and work productively. When someone asks how we are these days, the response can often sound a bit like a cry for help. Does this sound familiar?

> *"Hey, how are you?"*
>
> *"Oh, I'm just so busy. How are you?"*
>
> *"Yeah, same here."*

This common interaction indicates that we are constantly in *action* but rarely getting any *traction* in our attempts to live successful, satisfying, and impactful leadership lives. So, what to do?

Slowing Down to Go Fast

As Jack Johnson sings, the key to using time as a resource, rather than viewing it as a roadblock, is in our capacity to stay aware of the need to slow down. In this instance, I am not referring to *doing* less but to *being* less. To unleash the true dynamo in all of us, we need to live in the present, let go of our more harmful habits, and put ourselves first. It's only then we can establish, regain, or develop our focus, control, and energy levels.

In this chapter, we explore how twenty-one quick but powerful self-awareness levers will help reconceptualize what being a dynamo means for you in your leadership. In turn, the dynamo will come to represent how your relationship with time can create more energy rather than deplete it. Before we do, let's dig a little deeper into how our view of time can contribute to our relationship with it.

Time May Not Be the Problem

In truth, as I alluded to earlier, I have been grappling with overcoming limits on my time for years. Unlike other more sudden moments that helped define newer and more effective ways of thinking for me in my leadership roles, this one has been more accumulative. Almost every time, however, the result of feeling distress over a lack of time has led to lower levels of energy, drive, and productivity for me. This is compounded by living in times, as Johann Hari (2022) argues, where our focus is being stolen through a global crisis of diminishing collective attention. He writes that this is leading to diminished concentration spans for us all, which means that taking control of how we manage our time has become a tall order. This has certainly been a challenge for me, even though this admission may surprise some of those I've worked with.

It is true that many things—including unrealistic demands, poor working conditions, ineffective leadership practices, change fatigue, lack of resources, poor job satisfaction, and inequitable working conditions—contribute to the difficulties of effectively (and happily) managing time. In fact, in a Monash University study focusing on the perceptions of teachers and teaching in Australia, a whopping 75 percent of teachers found their workload to be unmanageable (Heffernan, Longmuir, Bright, & Kim, 2019). The American Federation of Teachers (AFT, 2022) carried out over two thousand interviews with educators about well-being, working conditions, and stressors. Up to 79 percent of those polled were dissatisfied with their jobs, an increase of 34 percent since the onset of the pandemic. These educators cited safety, workload, and political and workplace conditions as some of the factors that contributed to this (AFT, 2022). It is clear that with increasing stressors contributing to the profession, it is more important than ever for educators to look out for their own well-being as well as that of others. However, I would be doing you a disservice if, in this chapter, I focused on all the elements that sit outside your control. Instead, I will explore those things that we do have control over and can devote our energy to.

So, what helped me learn to slow down? My coaching practice has become my greatest teacher. Many of the people I work with—my *coachees*, let's call them—talk with me about the implications of working in high-stress environments where change is constant, demands are high, responsibilities increase, and other people both help and harm. What has struck me over a long period now is that each time my coachees would show up, they look increasingly tired, flat, and without energy. Over time, I have also learned to recognize this in myself.

While my coachees and I identified that insufficient time and support were often major causes of distress in their job, it became evident that the issue of energy—or lack thereof—was just as important. I started to wonder about the relationship between depletion of energy and our capacity to manage time effectively. It turns out there is a close link between the two. In fact, it may be that time isn't the enemy at all; rather, it's our inability to manage our energy.

As I've read more, asked more, and experienced more, I've discovered there are a lot of things that can work for us. What it comes down to is discarding the expectation that to be dynamic, we must always be in control, multitask, move at a hundred miles an hour, put out multitudes of spot fires, and still do our jobs at the highest level. Rather, we should take a different perspective and instead imagine a dynamic person as someone who is organized, focuses for longer periods of time, and harnesses their thinking to embrace slowness as a way of speeding up. Taking this approach, the dynamo can also maintain the discipline to minimize distractions in a way that fuels their energy levels as well as the energy levels of those around them.

I know it sounds all very abstract, but there are some very practical ways you can move toward becoming this type of dynamo—provided you're willing to examine how you manage your body, mind, and emotional and spiritual energy. This shift in focus from time to energy has helped me do the following.

- Expand my concentration levels (including for the writing of this book) by reducing my propensity to seek distraction.

- Work with and accept my emotions without having them define me or drain my energy (including in situations such as being let down by a colleague).

- Tune into my physiological triggers to elevate my self-awareness and not let these triggers disturb my focus (for example, by not reacting to an unwanted email or unmet expectations).

- Spend more time doing the things that nourish me (such as playing tennis with my son or reading a book from start to finish), leading to less resentment for the time I actually spend working.

- Accept that the world is constantly becoming more skilled at stealing my focus (especially through digital disruption), enabling me to be more kind to myself when I find myself giving in to temptation.

- See time as a precious resource that simply can't be wasted on things that sit outside what I believe and value most, both at work and at home.

Let's now take a deeper dive into recognizing whether your management of time is providing you with unwanted stress or limiting your leadership capacity. Then we'll move on to what you can do about it, using strategies that have helped countless people, including myself.

The Dynamo's Pain Points

Want to understand how to unleash the dynamo within? First, it's important to recognize some of the barriers that may be stopping such a dynamo from emerging. These factors seem most common in middle leaders who juggle numerous responsibilities, deal with shifting sands, and must be so many things to so many people across the hierarchy of their organizations. Maybe you can see yourself in some of the pain points I'll outline in the coming pages. As you read, think about which of these pain points contribute the most to your declining energy levels—and your capacity to manage time effectively.

I Can't Be Bothered

This pain point comes from leaving tasks undone because we simply don't feel like doing them. We may see them as too hard, uninteresting, or monotonous. This leaves us feeling less motivated and with depleted levels of energy to give to our work, in turn placing even greater pressure on ourselves by not giving tasks the time they need.

It Can Wait

Hello, procrastination! This happens when we put off a task until the clock counts down and there is little time to finish it. This can also come about through developed habits (I always cleaned the house when it came time to write student reports—it used to glisten at both the midpoint and end of the year), a lack of clarity on the task itself, or an overwhelming need to get things right (more on that later). When we experience this feeling, it becomes difficult to get into the flow, affecting our energy levels as we lose focus on what needs to be done.

There's Not Enough Time

This occurs when we feel the weight of having too much to do and not enough time to do it. It's definitely a common pain point for the leaders I coach in many different contexts, particularly when they place equal importance on many of the tasks they need to do, making prioritizing feel more difficult. This may also come about when we have many less important tasks to do at once, leading to overwhelm.

I'll Just Get It All Done Now

When we feel like there isn't enough time, we often commit to just getting it all done in a short window to get the tasks out of our hair. More research is emerging to discuss the disadvantages, both to time management practices and to our well-being, of trying to multitask like this. *Multitasking*, which is when we try to deal with more than one task at a time, means things take longer to be completed, as they can overwhelm our capacity to make decisions. A lack of sufficient focus on the task at hand can also result in poorer outcomes and increase the likelihood of mistakes. As researchers Kevin P. Madore and Anthony D. Wagner (2019) put it, "multitasking is almost always a misnomer, as the human mind and brain lack the architecture to perform two or more tasks simultaneously."

Sure, I Can Do That

On other occasions, the pleaser in us (see chapter 5, page 55) may mean we enthusiastically accept new tasks, only to find the time it takes to do the task is greater than the time available. This can lead to us feeling overwhelmed and resentful and engaging in more multitasking just to get it done.

I'm So Tired

Many of the pain points the dynamo can feel have other, unhelpful implications. For example, they may sleep less each day because they go through tasks without taking breaks or getting enough rest. The stress may also make getting to sleep harder, which can affect our capacity to concentrate and manage our workload. In William D. S. Killgore's (2010) study on the effects of sleep deprivation on cognition, the author found it can impair attention, working memory, and decision making, among other cognitive functions. This lack of sleep can ultimately diminish our capacity to perform well in our teaching and leadership work.

I'm So Disorganized

Being surrounded by clutter and mess can contribute to a feeling of being out of control. Think of your desk right now. As we used to joke in the staff room, are you more of a *piler* or *filer*? When we become disorganized, and can't find that piece of paper, time management practices are impeded. The same goes for the desktop of our computer. If it's a mess, we waste time searching for items and switching between tasks, again disrupting our capacity to use our time well. You may ask, What about those who prefer mess and being in a state of disorganization? Well, that's all well and good, I suppose, as long as that person isn't feeling the ill effects of not having enough time, and the subsequent distress it can bring themselves and potentially others.

I Just Need to Check My Emails

In his important book *Stolen Focus: Why You Can't Pay Attention—and How to Think Deeply Again*, Johann Hari (2022) cites the findings of a study by Gloria Mark (González & Mark, 2004)—and they're frightening. He states that Mark "observed how long on average an adult working in an office stays on one task. It was three minutes" (Hari, 2022, p. 8). Distractions may include socializing, digital device time (hang on, let me just check my emails for the hundredth time today!), and other less important tasks such as grabbing a snack from the pantry or checking the weather. The list really is endless, but sometimes we may not even notice our levels of distraction. This often leads to the inevitable thought: *There is never enough time in the day.*

Side note: I just checked my emails on my phone—proving once again that many authors really do write about what they are seeking for themselves!

I Don't Know Where to Start

While this statement often comes from an honest place, it has the potential to spill over into excuse land. An essential skill of managing time is our ability and commitment to prioritize. To complicate this, other people will often have different views about what is important. To-do lists that become too full also can compound pressure rather than alleviate it. I know many middle leaders understand the importance of prioritizing, but the biggest challenge is committing to it by creating habits that work for them.

It's Not Good Enough

These thoughts can be time suckers. When there is an overemphasis on detail (the trees) because we want to get things perfect, we can easily lose sight of the forest. These sorts of thoughts are a symptom of perfectionism, and they interfere with our time when the detail we're focusing on doesn't really impact the outcome. Perfectionism can spill over into inflexible planning approaches that don't honor the imperfections of people and processes, ultimately leading to frustration.

At the start of this chapter, I described the dynamo as someone who is organized, focuses for long periods of time, and harnesses their thinking to embrace slowness as a way of speeding up. They can also summon the discipline to minimize distractions in a way that fuels their energy levels and the energy levels of those around them. By recognizing where some of your pain points may be, you're now halfway to embracing your inner dynamo. The rest of this journey involves exploring how to overcome these pain points by incorporating self-awareness and habits that can make a genuine difference to your management of time.

Self-Awareness Levers to Overcome the Dynamo's Pain Points

These self-awareness levers are designed to assist you in becoming more conscious of the habits you can employ to overcome the perils of time. I have connected these self-awareness levers to the thoughts (described in the previous section) they are specifically designed to combat. While they may be useful tips, they are only as effective as the habits they end up becoming. Outside of self-awareness, any newly formed habit requires practice and experiences of success, so I will help you with that as part of the emerge exercise later in this chapter. Remember that many things we read or learn about aren't necessarily new. The real shift comes when we move from *I know this* to *I'm doing this*.

I Can't Be Bothered

The self-awareness levers for this pain point include zero in and relate it to the reward.

1. Zero In

Feeling uninspired? Find just one aspect of the work that you are interested in and concentrate on this as your starting point. For example, when I used to write student reports, I would always start with the personal development comment because the whole child's development was always more interesting to me than their mastery of a particular standard.

2. Relate It to the Reward

Think about how your work could assist you to achieve a separate but related objective that is significant to you. For example, in moments of low motivation while writing this book, I have thought about how research on particular topics will assist me to overcome a real pain point in my life.

It Can Wait

The self-awareness levers for this pain point include chunk it up, break it down, and establish a benefit blueprint.

3. Chunk It Up

Set a timer—if you're using your phone, turn all email notifications off!—and start working. It may be for just thirty minutes or an hour, for example. You may discover your momentum lasts beyond the timer and you just keep going. If not, set a new timer and give yourself a break. You may want to reward yourself with something once you have achieved the time. This form of chunking helps decrease the feeling of overwhelm while also building productivity.

4. Break It Down

Breaking tasks down can also make them seem more manageable. It could be setting aside five minutes to break the task down into chunks or attainable goals with suggested times so that you can see how it can realistically be done. If you feel it will help, you could then commit these to a calendar. I use this technique for the writing of books, reports, and articles.

5. Establish a Benefit Blueprint

Before you start a task, write down the benefits of completing it and use this as the blueprint for challenging your procrastination habits. Start with this question: What do I gain from getting this done? List the benefits and, if it helps to keep them visible, add them to your daily phone reminders until you get the task done. We are more likely to commit to things we see value in.

There's Not Enough Time

The self-awareness levers for this pain point include eliminate, automate, delegate, ideate, and concentrate; delegate, expect, and assume; and collaborate to mitigate.

6. Eliminate, Automate, Delegate, Ideate, and Concentrate

This tip has had a profound impact on me since being introduced to it at a business conference by keynote speaker Glenn Gerreyn. In essence, when we are given a task (particularly bigger projects), we should go through the following process: eliminate, automate, delegate, ideate, and concentrate (EADIC). This helps to ensure we don't waste copious amounts of time doing things we didn't need to do in the first place. An effective way of doing this is drawing five boxes, one for each stage in the EADIC process (as shown in figure 8.1, page 108). Then, write in each task associated with the job and decide if it can be eliminated, automated, delegated, ideated, or concentrated on. The questions in figure 8.1 will guide you through that process.

7. Delegate, Expect, and Assume

When we are strapped for time, delegating tasks to those we trust can be an option. The delegate, expect, and assume strategy, drawn from *Five Ways of Being*, which I wrote with Jane Danvers and Heather De Blasio (Danvers, De Blasio, & Grift, 2021), can assist you in doing this without shirking responsibility. Once you

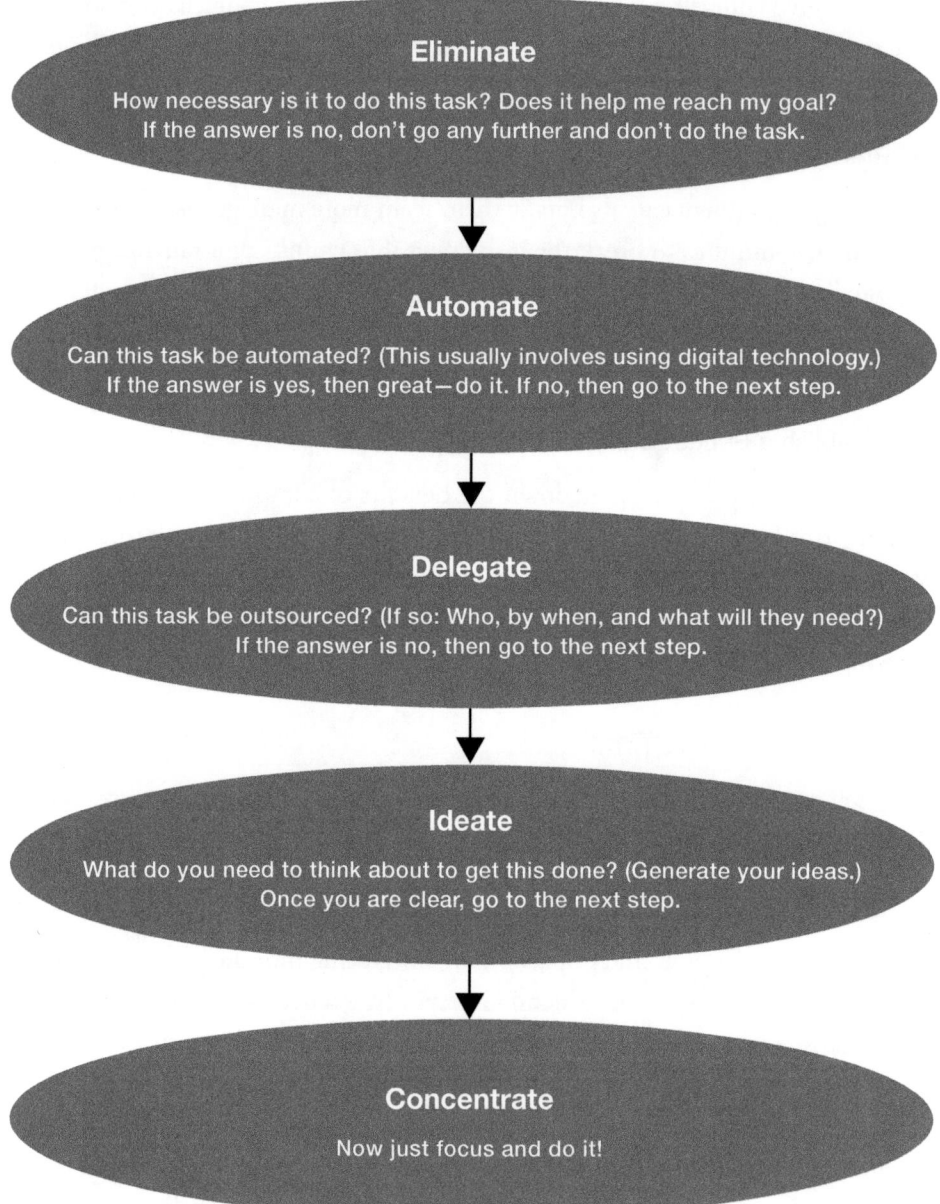

Figure 8.1: Making the most of every minute flowchart.

have clearly delegated a task, expect it will be done successfully by linking the task to that person's own motivations for wanting to assist. Assume that they can and will do a great job with your support.

8. Collaborate to Mitigate

Are there certain tasks that can be carried out with others? A problem shared is a problem halved, and the same can be said for the time it takes to get things done. This strategy works best when there is a common goal for all those involved, ensuring commitment.

I'll Just Get It All Done Now

The self-awareness levers for this pain point include apps off! and use calendars, not lists.

9. Apps Off!

Turn off most if not all notifications on your phone, computer, and other devices. Don't allow these digital devils to steal your focus and siphon off the energy required to lead responsibly and effectively. They are the silent killer for focus, but they can be easily eliminated with a little foresight. For example, you might use apps such as Freedom (https://freedom.to), SPACE (https://bit.ly/3U49gEd), and AppDetox (https://appdetox.github.io), which make apps of your choosing inaccessible so you can concentrate.

10. Use Calendars, Not Lists

Are your lists becoming as long as a roll of toilet paper? A better option is to mark out time in your calendar (I use Google calendar) by first estimating how long you will need to complete a task and then protecting this time. You will need to be strong and say no to other things that may crop up. Where possible, develop a criterion for the reasons you would be accessible at these times.

Sure, I Can Do That

This pain point has one self-awareness lever: take stock.

11. Take Stock

This one is simple in theory, but it's hard to execute. Before accepting any task that is optional, pause and offer the statement, "Let me get back to you. I have to check what commitments I have first, but I appreciate you asking me." Then consider all your current commitments, including the time they will take, before deciding whether to commit. This becomes more important when the task you are being asked to do is something you would like to do.

I'm So Tired

The self-awareness levers for this pain point include take short, sharp rests; practice healthy sleep hygiene; and concern, consult, and care.

12. Take Short, Sharp Rests

Anyone got a hammock I could lie in for five minutes? If only! Name some quick ways to take time out and even add these ideas to your calendar (or list, if you prefer). You could take one minute every hour to step outside and have a few deep breaths. You could even go for a five-minute walk, in- or outside the building, for no other purpose than to take a break. There are plenty of options, and the only real thing stopping you is your own capacity to make a more conscious choice to take those breaks.

13. Practice Healthy Sleep Hygiene

There is a growing body of evidence that a healthy sleep routine helps us thrive amid the demands of our busy lives (Suni, 2023). Given the importance of sleep hygiene, I encourage you to research practical ideas about how you might do this. For me, having a regular bedtime of 11:00 p.m., leaving my phone out of the bedroom, and getting some form of exercise each day has helped. Visit https://bit.ly/4cV4yBz for some other helpful tips.

14. Concern, Consult, and Care

If you're really concerned with your sleep patterns or have issues that no lifestyle changes can address, consult a professional to take care of your personal and professional well-being. Remember that a lot of our struggles with managing time center on our energy levels, and there could be some medical reasons impeding your capacity.

I'm So Disorganized

This pain point has one self-awareness lever: keep, trash, or fling.

15. Keep, Trash, or Fling

Whether you need to tidy up your digital workspace or overhaul your desk (or your life!), this simple but powerful strategy can help you. Simply organize everything through the lens of keep, trash, or fling. This is what it looks like.

- **Keep:** What must I keep as part of my job? (Decide where to put it.)
- **Trash:** What is not needed to do my job? (Throw it in the trash.)

- **Fling:** What might be needed to do my job? (Fling this somewhere for future reference, but don't use this one as an excuse to keep everything!)

I Just Need to Check My Emails

The self-awareness levers for this pain point include use headphones, close your door, and silence the enemy.

16. Use Headphones

Simple yet effective, using headphones at appropriate times can really help to distraction-proof your environment. A little like how noise-canceling headphones minimize the sound of hurtling through the air at hundreds of miles an hour when you're on a plane, this simple tip could help you to focus in ways you haven't before. Obviously, you will need to be aware of your workplace's policies, and it might not be the best look if you're teaching in the classroom—although I promise it will block out the noise! Seriously, though, I do use headphones when researching, reading online, or, at times, writing—all important aspects of most middle leadership job descriptions.

17. Close Your Door

I'm often surprised by how many leaders I work with who don't close their door. Perhaps it's the pleaser in them wanting to show they're available to solve problems and ensure they're accessible to their colleagues. This is important and admirable; however, it's unnecessary to leave the door open at all times. If we want to conserve energy, blocking out times where we close the door and focus, rather than constantly putting out spot fires for others, is at least of equal importance. You might even be able to build in that five-minute rest period to take a well-earned breath.

Of course, if you don't have an office door or the shared space you occupy renders this strategy impossible, you may need to employ a *no-disruption time* mantra. Finding a private location, booking an office space, or just simply letting people know you are not to be interrupted may help you shut the metaphorical office door.

18. Silence the Enemy

When possible, place your phone and all other digital devices out of reach. At the very least, put them where you must get up and move from your seat to get them. Make sure they are silenced or turned off completely, and organize other ways to receive information you deem critical. When I travel, I will often leave my phone in the bottom of my carry-on bag when at the airport to resist the urge to check emails and messages. This just makes it harder to access mindlessly. I let people know I can't be reached and will check when I get to the other side. Many people will make excuses and not do this, but the fact is it is still a choice. You just have to be willing to let go of the implications of doing so.

I Don't Know Where to Start

The self-awareness levers for this pain point include seek and destroy and prioritize with templates.

19. Seek and Destroy

When you're unsure what to prioritize or feel completely overwhelmed, seek counsel. A trusted mentor can assist you in your decision-making processes as you grapple with where to spend the most time and help you destroy those pesky feelings of anxiety that can take over and drain us of energy. Your trusted mentor should be someone you look up to because they seem to handle their workload well and always get things done in a timely and calm manner.

20. Prioritize With Templates

Scour the internet for the most useful templates available to help you organize your thoughts. Eisenhower's priority matrix, which we explored in chapter 6 (page 69), is one of the best-known task management templates. As touched on earlier, this matrix allows you to organize your tasks into four categories in decreasing order of priority, each with a corresponding course of action and timeframe (MindTools, n.d.).

1. Important and urgent (do these tasks right away)
2. Not urgent but important (decide when to do these tasks)
3. Not important but urgent (delegate these tasks if possible)
4. Not important or urgent (set these tasks aside to do later)

It's Not Good Enough

This pain point has one self-awareness lever: clarify the difference between high need and low need.

21. Clarify the Difference Between High Need and Low Need

Using a simple T-chart, look at the tasks at hand and identify all the elements that you believe will require the greatest focus and effort because the outcome depends on the quality of those elements. List these on the lefthand side of your chart under the heading High Need. On the other side, list those that don't need the same level of diligent care under the heading Low Need. As an example, consider figure 8.2, which outlines and prioritizes the thinking required to plan a leadership retreat.

High Need	Low Need
• Get budget.	• Transportation types and companies
• Formulate retreat agenda outline.	• Communication platforms
• Clear outcomes.	• Quality of in-house invitations
• Send out invites and date options.	• Overly sharing planning progress
• Get feedback and ideas.	• Details in the agenda
• Source venue and location.	
• Be prepared to be flexible.	

Figure 8.2: Leadership retreat planning T-chart.

Finding ways to reconceptualize the dynamo within can help us feel more in control. We learn how to slow down to go quick, and through this process, alleviate some of the stresses that may be stumbling blocks for us. Seeing the tangible progress we are making resolves some of the fear that can be associated with not getting things done.

We may also find ourselves with more time in our days. This is likely to lead to less resentment of the time (and energy) our jobs can extract, creating greater opportunity to focus on those things that are more important. This assists us in setting aside the more trivial aspects of our work that can rob us of the time to do things that have the greatest impact. We can also achieve individual and team goals in shorter lengths of time but with greater satisfaction and fulfillment. Who doesn't want that?

Emerge Exercises: The Self-Work

Not sure what to zero in on? Completing the following template (figure 8.3, page 114) will help you to gain clarity about where you should focus your attention. As you consider each pain point, tick the box that best fits your view of how often you experience it. If you're unsure, or want to elevate the accuracy of your self-awareness, ask someone else for their thoughts. Then write down what you might do with that knowledge, basing your response to each stem on your learning and reflections from this chapter.

Pain Point	I Think This Way . . .		
	Never	Sometimes	Often
I can't be bothered.			
Knowing this, I will . . .			
It can wait.			
Knowing this, I will . . .			
There's not enough time.			
Knowing this, I will . . .			
I'll just get it all done now.			
Knowing this, I will . . .			
Sure, I can do that!			
Knowing this, I will . . .			
I'm so tired.			
Knowing this, I will . . .			
I'm so disorganized.			
Knowing this, I will . . .			
I just need to check my emails.			
Knowing this, I will . . .			
I don't know where to start.			
Knowing this, I will . . .			
It's not good enough.			
Knowing this, I will . . .			

Figure 8.3: Toward action template.

By taking action to develop better time-management habits, build routines, and prioritize what truly matters, we can enjoy the benefits of letting go of constant demands. Instead of being driven by fear and anxiety, we can find a sense of peace and purpose in the present moment, knowing that we are making the most of our limited time on this earth. We can learn to disable the effects of time by focusing less on external demands and more on internal ones. The key to doing this is knowing you can change your relationship with time by changing some habits (like those listed in figure 8.3) and rejecting the premise that your life can start when you have got everything done—that's simply untrue, and it's a recipe for perpetual despondency. As Oliver Burkeman (2021) explains in his illuminating book *Four Thousand Weeks* (approximately the number of weeks in an eighty-year human life):

> There is a very down-to-earth kind of liberation in grasping that there are certain truths about being a limited human from which you'll never be

liberated. You don't get to dictate the course of events. And the paradoxical reward for accepting reality's constraints is that they no longer feel so constraining. (p. 109)

> **emerge**
> As a result of your learning here, what will you remind yourself of when that feeling of dread, associated with not having enough time, resurfaces?

Time management is a misnomer; the challenge is to manage ourselves.
—Stephen R. Covey

CHAPTER 9

The Judge and Juror: Overcoming Difficult People at Work

'Cause you can't judge a book by its cover . . .
Oh, take a different look

—Stevie Wonder, Henry Cosby, & Sylvia Moy

How can we overcome the problem of working with difficult people? First, we may need to challenge ourselves to take a look at what we mean by the term *difficult people*. Thinking of people as difficult is a slippery slope that often ends with a crash landing. The best leaders I have had understand this. Are people difficult or are they just different from us and see things differently from how we do? Are they deliberately annoying or have we just not yet learned and practiced ways to work with them? The answers to these questions depend on how we define *difficult*.

Difficult people are often referred to in this way because they have characteristics or personality traits that make it hard for us to communicate with them. Other terms I come across in my work to describe difficult people include *blockers*, *resisters*, *demanding*, *uncooperative*, and *painful*—to name just a few! I know people would have said similar things about me (if not worse). No one is perfect. We tend to become difficult when our needs aren't being met, we feel we aren't being listened to, we don't understand, we don't feel valued, we're tired and stressed, we don't see the point in something, we are out of our depth, or we aren't self-aware enough. Just stop for a moment and think of a time this may have been true for you.

It's easier to see others, rather than ourselves, as difficult. However, we can grow our capacity to empathize with those we find most difficult. Our ability to work effectively with all types of people to maintain and develop healthy work environments is a critical skill for middle leaders to harness. So, rather than thinking of people as difficult, it may serve you better to think about them as people you are having some difficulties with. As Stevie Wonder sings in his classic song, when we do this, we lessen the propensity to judge a book by its cover, and instead look for deeper personal connections and common ground. Through this shift in perspective, we can open ourselves up to the very people we call difficult and begin the process of learning to work together.

Taking a Different Look

The longer you are in leadership, the more likely it is that you will be confronted with the many difficulties associated with a person's way of being. The intensity of these difficulties will vary depending on the person and situation. This can bring distress or opportunity, depending on how you approach it.

When you take on the role of judge and juror, you draw conclusions about someone that close the case and offer no opportunity for recourse. Just calling someone difficult or a blocker in some ways has meant the judge and juror in you have already given their verdict. And that puts you on the back foot. The key to leading people you experience difficulties with rests in your capacity to suspend judgment—and we do all make judgments. In that space of temporary neutrality, you must examine your own intentions and behaviors. With elevated self-awareness, you can then make decisions that are more likely to strengthen your relationship and facilitate your influence and impact.

We tend to develop our identities as leaders by looking to other leaders who we respect and admire. One of my early leaders taught me a lot about working with difficult people and how we can keep our propensity to act as judge and juror at bay. In this chapter, you will learn some ways to take a different look at some of the difficulties we have with people and what we can do about them.

Difficult Dianne

In the early days of my coaching career, I was working with a brand-new school. My role was to support the development of the school's collaborative culture to benefit staff and students in their learning. I met with all staff members and got to know the team that I'd be working with. I thoroughly enjoyed the excitement and prospect of establishing a new culture. Then, slowly, the whispers started as everyone got to know each other a little more. I started to hear conversations about other people, and a lot of them seemed to center on Dianne. I gradually realized that every time

Dianne's name was mentioned, some of my colleagues would roll their eyes. Deep breaths would be drawn, and, in some cases, some disrespectful things were said. Dianne became the unspoken "difficult" one. Just pause for a moment and think—have you ever come across anyone painted with the same brush? Have you ever been perceived that way? These are not necessarily pleasant things to confront, but they are important.

Sadly, this scenario was relatively common in many of the organizations I have worked with. It's always covert, but you'll find it if you just scratch the surface. People congregate to share in their frustrations about working with someone and unwillingly, and perhaps unknowingly, contribute to a toxic culture, or at least to pockets of toxicity. This erodes the relational trust that's vital to the success of an organization. Further, Brené Brown (2022) reminds us of the perils of using the shortcomings of another person as a focus for building relationships with others: "Nothing that celebrates the humiliation or pain of another person builds lasting connection" (p. 34). A misguided attempt at building connection through the shared frustrations of working with a colleague becomes the norm—and that's not constructive.

Back to Dianne. As the year rolled on, I began to work with Dianne, and I did find her a bit difficult. She seemed reserved and a little removed from some of collaborative contexts. She wasn't the easiest person to talk to, and I would often spend a little longer with her than I was used to with others, explaining to her aspects of the work. I did notice very quickly that she had a genuine passion for teaching, and I detected in her a sadness that maybe others hadn't. They certainly hadn't discussed it with me. Without even really realizing, I watched the principal and his way of being with her. He treated her with respect; he listened and asked her questions. When challenged by some of the things that she said, even publicly, he would bring the discussion back to common ground, namely the mission of the school that each person was bound to, so that it never got personal. He kept an open-door policy with her (when he wasn't enforcing the close your door strategy I mentioned in the previous chapter, page 111) and never engaged in any workplace gossip. This resulted in Dianne growing professionally in significant ways. She stayed at the school for longer than she had in any previous job. She also improved in her performance, which benefited both students and those colleagues she worked with directly.

As I learned more about Dianne, it became apparent that through the course of her work at this school, she was struggling through a very difficult divorce. She had also come from a school where her trust "bucket" was left very empty, so she remained guarded. Unlike me, most of her experiences in education with leaders were negative ones, and she had high levels of resentment when arriving at this school. (She was placed there by the system rather than making the choice herself.) So, all in all, Dianne had lower levels of trust, success, confidence, and self-belief than most of the people she worked with. Combined with her personal situation, many of the difficulties people found when working with her came from the very difficulties Dianne was experiencing in herself.

This was an important lesson for my own leadership. Except for the principal, other leaders seemed to compound the difficulties rather than work through them. This principal taught me the power of suspending judgment, demonstrating respect, communicating differences respectfully, and stating beliefs consistently and with kindness, while never deviating from the mission of the organization and expecting all others to do the same. He was looking at Dianne differently from the others and it showed.

The Judge and Juror's Pain Points

There are many ways people can make life difficult for us. We might work with people who are lazy (or at least not as hardworking as us), highly dependent or too independent, different in their approach, resentful, despondent, lacking clarity, dishonest, or little interested in aspects of the work or their role. They may try to wrestle control from you, say too little, or just not do what they've been asked. They may gossip harmfully or protect their territory as though their life depends on it. I could go on, but you get the point. To get the most out of this chapter, read it with someone in mind who you find hard to work with.

It is important to know what the pain points and intentions are of those who are causing us difficulties because that knowledge provides us with insights into how to deal with them. As Sanjay Raosaheb Biradar, R. G. Dhole, B. P. Jadhav, and Vinod Devidas Devarkar (2010) remind us, "By understanding what people expect to gain from using undesirable behaviours, we are in a much better position to deflect and defeat the difficult behaviour and move the person from problem identification to problem-solving" (p. 6).

Navigating whatever the difficulty is requires us to move outside of our own thoughts and feelings and seek further information about the other person to better understand them. We put away the judge and juror, who have already condemned them to the land of difficult people, and instead embrace the inquirer within to explore. It can be helpful to draw on the fields of personality, adult development, and change theory to better recognize and overcome some of the pain points associated with working with difficult people, which include not understanding your people, not appreciating the complexity of adult development, and not understanding that people come before process.

Not Understanding Your People

It's possible you just don't know the intentions of the person creating the difficulty, which means you're making assumptions. The problem with assumptions is that they aren't facts—just things we believe to be true. We tend to spend more time with people who think more like us because it is easier; we don't have to exert so much energy being aware of ourselves in the moment by watching our words. With trusted colleagues, it is different. We trust them because they demonstrate personal regard, integrity, competence, and respect (Bryk & Schneider, 2002). They also keep confidentiality. While it may be a challenge, that is also what those difficult people want from us.

What do different personality styles want to gain by being difficult? We may not find all the answers by understanding different personality styles. But as we learn more about what people want, we can at the very least broaden and deepen our empathy levels. In my work with collaborative teams, I have found it useful to consider the DiSC® model, which identifies the following four primary emotions that drive people and their subsequent behavior.

- **D**ominance: direct, strong-willed, and forceful (fast-paced and skeptical)
- **I**nfluence: sociable, talkative, and lively (fast-paced and accepting)
- **S**teadiness: gentle, accommodating, and soft-hearted (moderate-paced and accepting)
- **C**onscientiousness: private, analytical, and logical (moderate-paced and skeptical; Intégro Learning Company, n.d.)

Depending on which style or styles you resonate with most, you might find it difficult to work with colleagues at a slower or faster pace or who are too accepting or skeptical for you. The polarity is interesting and may give you some insights, and there are many books, websites, and training programs that can help you with that. What is most useful here is how these explanations help us to understand the intentions of others. Let's take a closer look.

Dominance

For dominators, it is all about control. They do not want to lose ground or be taken advantage of. Under too much pressure or confrontation, they can display combative behaviors and compete for power. Given their competitive nature, if they don't get immediate results, find solutions to problems, gain some power or control, or see how the work aligns with their own views on what is needed, you may find them quite hard to work with.

What might dominators hope to gain when being difficult? Power, control, social status, and influence.

Influence

Influencers fear social rejection. They are social creatures who enjoy attention and interaction. Given they are naturally empathetic, they can lose their confidence and direction when under pressure and revert to worrying about what others think of them. This can affect their organization and capacity to get things done, making life for those who lead them potentially difficult.

What might influencers hope to gain when being difficult? Understanding, support, conversation, and direction.

Steadiness

The steadies don't embrace change. They do not like unclear direction, nonspecific tasks, and environments where they can't concentrate and get things done. They prefer repetition over shifting sands and listening over talking. They can become difficult for leaders by demonstrating martyrlike behaviors, going silent, or disengaging from interactions.

What might steadies hope to gain when being difficult? Direction, purpose, and certainty.

Conscientiousness

People who fit the conscientiousness profile don't like surprises. Being well prepared, thorough, and right are important to them. This means when they're under pressure or threatened, they may become more guarded and critical of ideas or others. Under pressure or when confronted with mediocrity or a lack of detail or evidence-based solutions, they might become intolerant to disparities and overly analytical of the work of others and the group.

What might conscientious people hope to gain when being difficult? Better results, more evidence or data, thorough planning, and the time to do things well.

What this can illuminate is an understanding of what people who are being difficult want from you. The more we can learn about what they are seeking, the more likely we are to be able to find ways to support them. There is a range of views on the impact that understanding different personalities can have, but as I mentioned in chapter 3 (page 35), understanding our personality traits and becoming more aware of them is important in our leadership. Provided we don't label ourselves (or others), we can use them to explore how we might navigate the difficulties of working effectively in human-based systems that require the highest levels of interdependence.

How might this help you with the difficult person I asked you to think about earlier in this chapter?

Not Appreciating the Complexity of Adult Development

The key to working with people you find difficult is empathy. As Michael Bungay Stanier (2020) points out, "Empathy is how you connect with the other person across from you. It's the act of seeing them fully, being present to who they are, and having that awareness then influence the way you respond to the world." However, while empathy is the critical ingredient for leaders to understand their people, Stanier (2020) goes on to say:

> It's easy to not have that connection in our lives. The combination of our neurobiology, our busy-ness, the nature of our organizations and even the nature of capitalism can lead us to default to seeing the other person as a role, a tool, a cog in the machine. You harden your heart so you can get things done.

What can help us keep from hardening our hearts and seeing people as more resource than human? From my experience, it's developing our awareness of the fact that adults, like children, develop at different rates for different reasons, and therefore they may need different things.

According to influential psychologist Robert Kegan (1983), becoming an adult is tied to the capacity to construct our reality through elevating our self-awareness so we can more consciously notice our beliefs and emotions. This would indicate that not everyone has the same level of self-awareness, nor do they focus on the same things (even by the same age). In his theory of adult development, Kegan (1983) proposes five stages, of which only the last three relate specifically to adults. What underpins his theory is the notion that as we develop, we shift in what we know from the subject (what is controlling us) to object (what we are controlling). Natali Morad (2017) sums up the two states in the following way:

- Subject ("I AM")—Self concepts we are attached to and thus cannot reflect on or take an objective look at. They include personality traits, assumptions about the way the world works, behaviors, emotions, etc.

- Object ("I HAVE")—Self concepts that we can detach ourselves from. That we can look at, reflect upon, engage, control and connect to something else.

Kegan's (1983) work is complex, but what it means in essence for working with difficult people is that everyone is on a journey to becoming more conscious of the impact that their thoughts, emotions, and actions have on both themselves and others. We find it inherently difficult when we lack the objectivity to distance ourselves from the challenges we experience with people, to reflect and take greater control of our thoughts, feelings, and actions. It is even harder when the person we are dealing with also lacks the capacity to see things more objectively.

Understanding the complexity of how adults develop can help us to see others more fully. And as we accept their imperfections and unique traits, our connection can be strengthened. We can then use this growing awareness to work more willingly with them and let go of the inclination to judge. All these elements have their roots in empathy.

How might this help you with the person you thought about earlier?

Not Understanding That People Come Before Process

It can be difficult for leaders to depersonalize the different reactions their colleagues can have through any process of change. This can apply to many changes, such as a new program being introduced or changes to district policy. But the fact is that everybody has different levels of concern for these proposed changes.

As humans, we tend not to embrace change until we see the value or benefit to ourselves and those we are responsible for. We often view change as more of an event than a process, which can limit our capacity to embrace the complexity associated with the change process. It is important for middle leaders to understand and see change as a process that requires them to monitor how their people are feeling about the change. This means they can address any difficulties that may surface before they become too hard to handle.

Gene E. Hall and Shirley M. Hord (2011) make a compelling case for using the Concerns-Based Adoption Model to legitimize people's personal concerns about change, honoring the fact that change is a personal experience and acknowledging there can be growth in the way people feel about change. Each of the seven stages of concern is accompanied by an expression of concern that summarizes how a person may be personally feeling about a particular change. There are many iterations of the model available on the internet, but I've provided an example in table 9.1. In this

Table 9.1: Stages of Concern

Stage of Concern	How the Concern Could Be Articulated	Associated Thoughts and Emotions
0. Unconcerned	I'm not concerned about this. I've seen it all before.	• Overwhelmed • Avoidant • Full of dread • Fearful • Apathetic • Stressed • Despairing • Contemptuous
1. Information	I'd like to know what the teaching constructs are.	• Confused • Reluctant • Curious
2. Personal	Will I have to change anything I do in the classroom?	• Worried • Inconvenienced • Apprehensive
3. Management	I am spending a lot of time on the self-assessment inventories.	• Engaged • Surprised • Open-minded • Prepared to integrate
4. Consequence	I can see the difference this is making to my students. If I just change this aspect, it will work even better. This is quite good.	• Hopeful • Joyful • Satisfied • Appreciative of value and relevance • Grateful • Relieved
5. Collaboration	How can I help my colleagues get the impact I am having from my focus?	• Giving • Connected • Compassionate • Supportive
6. Refocusing	I think I can do some other things that will make this even more impactful.	• Excited • Engaged • Proud • Full of wonder • Interested • Trusting

Source: Adapted from American Institutes for Research, 2010.

table, I have matched the stages of concern (starting from zero through to six) and my observations of how people have articulated their concern when I introduced the Teachers as Architects of Learning program to their school.

What I appreciate about this model is that it honors how different people think and feel through the *process* of change. This becomes an opportunity for leaders to depersonalize their responses when they perceive someone is being difficult. By focusing on how their colleagues are feeling to move them to the next stage, rather than focusing on what they are not doing, a leader can become less judgmental and more empathetic and increase their impact and influence.

As you might expect from looking at table 9.1, it is much easier to work with people who are at stage 4, 5, or 6 than those who are still at one of the first four. However, if we resist the urge to be judge and juror, we can understand that it's not that the person is being difficult; it's just that their needs in the change process are yet to be met or they can't see the benefits and impact the change might have in the way that you do. We can't, for example, make someone feel excited about using the Teachers as Architects of Learning program to strengthen their reflective practice when they feel dread. But we can honor how they feel, inquire about why they feel that way, and then help them access further information to alleviate that dread. By doing this, we help our people move through the stages of concern while also building a more trusting relationship.

How might this help you with the person you've been thinking of in this chapter?

Self-Awareness Levers to Overcome the Judge and Juror's Pain Points

There are ten levers that are useful when working with people who cause us difficulties, minimizing the unhelpful judgments we might be making toward ourselves and others. I call them dispositions, as my wish for you is that these levers will become ways in which you are predisposed to act.

The ten dispositions we will dig deeper into in this chapter include the following.

1. Depersonalize it.
2. Develop rapport.
3. Demand what's right.
4. Deepen your empathy.
5. Deploy self-regulation.
6. Don't take yourself too seriously.
7. Discover support networks.
8. Demonstrate compassion.

9. Display patience.
10. Devote yourself to letting go.

As with any new habit we try to form, it will take practice and commitment to operationalize one or more of these levers and turn them into dispositions. Think about the opportunities this will create in your leadership, as mentioned in chapter 2 (page 23), as you work toward being more conscious in your self-responses when people cause you distress. This is much better than reacting unconsciously, which has the potential to make situations worse for everyone.

Learning how to stay still in the moment as you navigate difficulties will set you in good stead:

> A mind that can stand still is a mind that has the quality of a rock, solid, unmoving. A rock is a better tool with which to penetrate a brick wall than jelly. A rock-like mind isn't going to disintegrate at the slightest impact.
> (Khema, 1987, p. 109)

Armed with some of the levers described in coming pages, you'll also be better placed to overcome such challenges.

1. Depersonalize It

Embracing the pause and allowing yourself to remain objective is critical to depersonalizing the thoughts, feelings, and actions of others. Engaging in neutral thinking (outlined in chapter 5, page 55) and pausing when talking with colleagues can build our capacity for objectivity. Pausing can take many forms, but giving yourself a moment before responding or after a colleague responds is a simple yet powerful way to practice this skill.

To do this, remind yourself that other people's responses and moods are not your responsibility. Staying true to what is important to you and the organization, as the principal did with Dianne in the example I shared earlier, assists you to do this. It also leads you to express your own thoughts and emotions in calm, considered, and concise ways, modeling the very professional behaviors we would hope to see in others.

2. Develop Rapport

Rapport is as much a feeling as it is a concept. When we are in rapport with people, there is a place in our minds where others live—and vice versa—no matter how temporary. As middle leaders, it is our job to consciously seek opportunities to develop a rapport with others, particularly those who we may find difficult. We must invest the time to get to know people beyond our assumptions to find out more earnestly what makes them tick. Showing your colleagues that you are genuine in your attempts to understand them aids compassion and care, which can in turn lead them to exercise more respectful ways of working with you.

We can consciously build rapport with others by leveraging our awareness to match (not mimic) language, posture, gestures, or tone. Think about how masterful some teachers are in building rapport with their students as they use their words, actions, and the environment to create psychologically safe places for their students to be vulnerable and to think at higher levels. The same principles apply here.

3. Demand What's Right

While this might sound a bit dramatic, there are times when we must stand our ground and express how we feel. We should never feel compromised when dealing with people whose behavior is inexcusable at worst and unprofessional at best. No one has a monopoly on respect—it's an entitlement for all.

One of the most effective ways to ensure we don't personalize a situation, while also managing to stand our ground, is to express how something makes us feel in a calm but assertive fashion. It may take bravery, because we can't control the response that we will get, but we will have left no shades of gray in expressing ourselves. Consider the difference between the following responses.

- **Assertive and fair (conscious):** "When you conduct yourself in that way, I feel disappointed for the impact it has on our capacity to deal with the matter at hand, and for the sake of the team, I really don't want to see it again."

- **Aggressive and unfair (unconscious):** "Can you just stop being such a complainer? No one likes it, and it wears thin on everyone here. For goodness's sake, just keep your mouth shut."

When we try for a conscious response (a response that is both assertive in its delivery and fair at its heart), we communicate our boundaries clearly by focusing on the professional impact of others' actions rather than our problem with their personality.

4. Deepen Your Empathy

We never really know what is happening in the minds of our colleagues. We have the inside information on ourselves only. As the story of Dianne highlights, there might be more going on, such as a relationship breakdown or the accumulation of previous traumatic experiences, that you are not privy to. Practicing our capacity to see things from different perspectives, being willing to have our assumptions challenged, listening intently (not just hearing), and elevating our self-awareness to remain objective are all game changers for the quest to lead with empathy.

5. Deploy Self-Regulation

In moments of emerging tension, think metaphorically about how you might raise your heart and not your hand. Losing the plot never looks or feels good, and it often comes with lasting implications for the building of relational trust.

Taking time to reflect on your thoughts and emotions through journaling can help you process and regulate them. Dedicate a specific time each day to put pen to paper and document your experiences, feelings, and reactions. This will enable you to gain insight into your emotions and develop a more balanced perspective. Engaging in physical exercise is another powerful tool for managing stress and promoting emotional regulation. Exercise releases endorphins, natural mood boosters that can help to reduce feelings of anxiety and depression (Mayo Clinic, 2022). Consider integrating regular exercise into your daily routine, such as going for a brisk walk or jog, taking a yoga class, or hitting the gym.

Practicing self-compassion is also crucial for managing difficult emotions. Treat yourself with the same kindness and empathy you would offer to a close friend. This might include indulging in self-care activities, like taking a relaxing bath (maybe not ideal when at school!), listening to music, or engaging in a favorite hobby. Self-compassion can help you feel more grounded and resilient in the face of challenging emotions.

The negative thoughts and deeds of others are not a justification for you to act in similar ways. It can be tempting to sound off to colleagues and vent to anyone who will care to listen, but of course, all we are achieving is taking the low road. Enable the professional in you to elevate your self-awareness as you think about the consequences of reacting rather than responding. The high road will be full of potholes, but it is more likely to lead you to your destination and will signify an open invitation to join you.

6. Don't Take Yourself Too Seriously

I try to take what I do seriously without taking *myself* too seriously, and I find when I succeed, it keeps me grounded, accessible, and satisfied. The chance to laugh and use humor is an important tool for leaders to use as they navigate difficult situations. We never want this to turn into flippancy, whereby people feel dismissed or ridiculed. However, if we can remind ourselves of the bigger picture, we will often find the lighter side of things, even in stressful situations. In their research on humor, Rod A. Martin and Thomas E. Ford (2018) identify humor as an important ingredient in relieving tension; they refer to this as *relief theory*. They compare it to an engine in which laughter can activate the pressure valve. This relieves us of the pent-up pressure and releases the energy built up through prolonged stress.

7. Discover Support Networks

Find out who is around to support you as you work hard at being the best you can be in support of others. It could be that you need support in a hard conversation or even an additional supportive presence at a meeting. Asking people you respect and admire for their insights can be worthwhile. Everyone has had difficulties working with people, even if they don't demonstrate them. Discuss your issues with someone higher up the chain by expressing your specific concerns. Keep the conversations professional by always focusing on how it affects the overall goals of the team or organization. Most likely they already know about the issue or have experienced similar difficulties themselves.

8. Demonstrate Compassion

The most compassionate people in life can still have bad days—even bad weeks or bad years. Life is full of challenges and hard times. That's inevitable. This is true for the people you work with too. There may be genuinely painful reasons for a change in someone's professional behavior. This doesn't mean we have to excuse the behaviors, but we do need to comprehend them. This relates to deepening our capacity for empathy and depersonalizing things. Compassion requires us to see beyond our own thoughts and feelings to understand someone else's and let that shape our words.

9. Display Patience

If practice makes perfect, then practicing patience brings contentment. Patience is our capacity to remain still (calm, considered, aware, and present) amid chaos. This chaos could include situations that lead us to frustration, bewilderment, exasperation, suffering, disillusionment, confusion, or even anger. The depth of the emotions we may feel will in part depend on how long we sit with and accept them. The key to displaying patience is catching your thoughts as they arise and learning how to set them aside. Keeping a larger frame of reference in mind can also help.

10. Devote Yourself to Letting Go

Letting go is learning to anchor yourself in the present. In the present, there is no past and no future, and we quiet the whispers that can drag us down and siphon off our energy. This requires devotion because it can't happen in an instant. It takes conscious practice and commitment, but when we build our capacity to let go, we spend less time on problem identification and more time on problem solving. It minimizes the risk of certain people or situations contaminating other areas of our day—in work and in life.

Think of letting go as a generous process of releasing the things we may have once held dear but are now getting in the way of achieving professional fulfillment, influence, and impact. Grant Hilary Brenner (2020) explains the ideal process like this: "Rather than 'breaking the pattern,' the pattern gradually softens and re-shapes itself. Letting go is more gentle, generous, and self-compassionate than coercively ripping away something dear."

In summary, the key to overcoming difficult people at work is to dispense with acting as judge and juror, and instead embrace a more nuanced, empathetic, and noble attitude. This shift helps everyone move from complaining to solving, talking to listening, undervaluing to valuing, and disempowering to empowering while also making sure we take care of both ourselves and our people.

Emerge Exercises: The Self-Work

Here at the end of this chapter, I want to take you back to the person or people you might find most difficult to work with and ask you to reflect. What has surfaced in this chapter that can assist you in overcoming the difficulties of working with them? How could this free you to focus on the more fulfilling, impactful aspects of your work? Use the following stems to help you process and record your thinking in your journal.

- As a result of reading this chapter, I think it's important to . . .
- I believe this will help me . . .
- It will help me to think . . .
- It will help me feel . . .

- It will help me do . . .
- It will help me to let go of . . .
- To strengthen my commitment to this, I will seek support from . . .

> **emerge**
>
> As a result of reading this chapter, what thoughts will you benefit from setting aside to work successfully with a wide variety of people?

If we can't see eye to eye, let's try heart to heart.

—Unknown

EPILOGUE

Coming Into View

I seem to have run in a great circle, and met myself again on the starting line.

—Jeanette Winterson

In the introduction, I explained that this book would support you in developing your self-awareness, and I asked you to consider using it to examine your leadership self. Now that we are concluding, I wonder what has emerged for you since you first started reading. As you've looked in the mirror and focused on the leader you see, what is different about the image in front of you, and what might you do with these insights? What is coming more clearly into view?

Looking Back to Move Forward

Maybe for you it's about tackling that difficulty that has seen you bury your head in the sand. It could be having a conversation that you've been avoiding because of your fear of being disliked. It might be spending less time focusing on how busy you are and more time on conserving your energy levels so you can be at your best. Perhaps it is focusing less on how others perceive you and more on what feels intuitively right for you. Possibly it's taking a different view of the people you find difficult to work with to learn more about them—and yourself.

Regardless of what your takeaways are, I hope they serve you well and you continue to use your growing self-awareness to overcome the inevitable pain points of leading. I want those pain points to become opportunities for your growth.

A Series of Starting Lines

I view our leadership lives as a series of starting lines in the sense described by the quote at the start of this epilogue from Jeanette Winterson's (1997) *Oranges Are Not the Only Fruit*. In some ways, it *should* feel like this because it means we are growing. Many of the pain points we will experience we will have felt before, and they will challenge us to revisit previous approaches and think about what they taught us. At these moments, we use the power of self-awareness to check in on our values, beliefs, mental state, motivations, personality traits, physiological responses, and the perceptions of others. As we do, we become more conscious of our unconscious selves, quieting the ego that often becomes a barrier in our quest to find the most beneficial ways to feel, think, say, and do in our leadership work.

This rang true for me while I was co-presenting an online leadership course based on *Five Ways of Being*, which I coauthored with Jane Danvers and Heather De Blasio (Danvers et al., 2021). As the minutes counted down to the start, I noticed that no one was joining the online space. With the starting time upon us, those who registered for the program were nowhere to be seen. I could feel the emotions rise in me as I became more flustered, worried, and agitated. Why weren't they there? My team was responsible for the registration process and making sure all those who signed up had everything they needed!

I checked my phone, having turned my notifications off earlier in the day (trying to practice what I preach in chapter 8, page 99), and there it was: a series of emails from the participants alerting our team to the fact they couldn't get in. Ten minutes had passed. My professional value of providing the best learning experiences was being compromised. My belief that providing people with the highest level of professionalism demonstrates that we value them was challenged. My emotions started to affect what I said to my colleagues and my team as we all scrambled to rectify the situation, and then it hit me. I paused, breathed, and observed my emotions—and I didn't like what I saw. I enlarged my frame of reference and thought about this moment as part of the bigger picture, and it helped. It was not a catastrophe—more of a hiccup. In that moment, I felt calmer and clearer. Eventually, the participants joined—fifteen minutes late, but present. I apologized, told the truth, and let them know how I felt and why it mattered. I showed them that I cared. We had a great session, and on the following day, they all came back for more (and on time).

Through heightened self-awareness, I had quieted my ego: the ego that starts with *I*. Only through my self-awareness was I able to quell my unconscious self, whose ego was running rampant. The unconscious narrative of thoughts such as *I can't believe this*, *I will need to let the team know how unhappy I am*, and *I thought they had this under control* were replaced with a more conscious narrative, featuring thoughts along the lines of *This is not a disaster*, *People will understand*, and *My team must feel horrible about this*.

Was it the first time I'd felt those emotions when things didn't go according to plan? Of course not! I'd been at that starting line before. Only this time, the race I ran had a more beneficial ending than many of my previous attempts. The reason I know this is that I asked my team and colleagues. I wanted to understand their perceptions of the situation and my handling of it. Otherwise, the accuracy of my own assumptions couldn't be confirmed. When I checked in, my team felt heard, valued, and understood (albeit stressed). My colleagues felt valued and appreciated. I felt more able to influence and impact to ensure this would be less likely to happen again through the calm and respectful approach I chose. The conscious leader in me emerged just when we needed it to, and through practice, I am sure it will continue to. We're all works in progress.

What I know for sure is that moments like these are littered through our days and weeks, and they present us with opportunities. They are our starting lines. When they do crop up, we have a choice. However, to make the choice that brings us fulfillment, impact, influence, connectedness, and the joy we seek as leaders, we will need to leverage our self-awareness. These levers will help us bring our egos (our unconscious selves) into view so that we can be conscious about what we do with our thoughts, emotions, and actions. The leaders and teachers who have had the greatest impact on my life understood this, and I hope that after reading this book, you will feel well placed to put your insights into practice.

Revisiting the starting line of this book, I mentioned that the word *emergence* represents when something appears from where nothing was. So, from the perspectives gained in reading this book, what opportunities have emerged that will help you become the leader you aspire to be? What blind spots have become visible to you in your ongoing pursuit of a gratifying professional life? And what is the value of their illumination?

Whatever the answers to those questions might be, I wish you well in applying them to the important work you do in service to yourself and others.

It is not the right advice that liberates, but the action based on it.
—Sri Nisargadatta Maharaj

References and Resources

American Federation of Teachers. (2022). *Under siege: The outlook of AFT members.* Accessed at www.aft.org/sites/default/files/media/2022/de-14326_aft_member_survey.pdf on March 21, 2024.

American Institutes for Research. (2010, December 8). *Stages of concern: Concerns-Based Adoption Model.* Accessed at www.air.org/resource/stages-concern-concerns-based-adoption-model on April 18, 2024.

American Psychological Association. (n.d.a). *Avoidance coping.* Accessed at https://dictionary.apa.org/avoidance-coping on March 21, 2024.

American Psychological Association. (n.d.b). *Confirmation bias.* Accessed at https://dictionary.apa.org/confirmation-bias on March 21, 2024.

Anicich, E. M., & Hirsh, J. B. (2017, March 22). *Why being a middle manager is so exhausting.* Accessed at https://hbr.org/2017/03/why-being-a-middle-manager-is-so-exhausting on March 21, 2024.

Aruba Ostrich Farm. (n.d.). *Facts: Get acquainted with ostriches.* Accessed at www.arubaostrichfarm.com/ostrich-facts/ on April 11, 2024.

Aurelius, M. (2006). *Meditations: The stoic philosophy of Marcus Aurelius* (G. Hays, Trans.). Mineola, NY: Dover.

Ayala, F. J. (2010). The difference of being human: Morality. *Proceedings of the National Academy of Sciences, 107*(suppl. 2), 9015–9022.

Baecher, L. (2012). Pathways to teacher leadership among English-as-a-second-language teachers: Professional development by and for emerging teacher leaders. *Professional Development in Education, 38*(2), 317–330.

Ballard, W. (n.d.). *Teachers make over a thousand decisions each day, and it's exhausting.* Accessed at www.boredteachers.com/post/teachers-make-four-decisions-per-minute on March 21, 2024.

Bass, B. M., & Yammarino, F. J. (1991). Congruence of self and others' leadership ratings of naval officers for understanding successful performance. *Applied Psychology, 40*(4), 437–454.

Bassett, M., & Shaw, N. (2018). Building the confidence of first-time middle leaders in New Zealand primary schools. *International Journal of Educational Management, 32*(5), 749–760.

Beck, J. (2016, November 23). *The running conversation in your head.* Accessed at www.theatlantic.com/science/archive/2016/11/figuring-out-how-and-why-we-talk-to-our-selves/508487 on March 21, 2024.

Beck, J. S. (2005). *Cognitive therapy for challenging problems: What to do when the basics don't work.* New York: Guilford Press.

Beck, J. S. (2011). *Cognitive behavior therapy: Basics and beyond* (2nd ed.). New York: Guilford Press.

Biradar, S. R., Dhole, R. G., Jadhav, B. P., & Devarkar, V. D. (2010). *Handling difficult people for better administration* [Paper presentation]. Shri Chhatrapati Shivaji College, Omerga, India.

Brach, T. (2004). *Radical acceptance: Embracing your life with the heart of a Buddha.* New York: Random House.

Bravata, D. M., Watts, S. A., Keefer, A. L., Madhusudhan, D. K., Taylor, K. T., Clark, D. M., et al. (2020). Prevalence, predictors, and treatment of impostor syndrome: A systematic review. *Journal of General Internal Medicine, 35*(4), 1252–1275.

Brenner, G. H. (2020, July 23). *5 keys to letting go: Recognizing pathological needs is hard, but it is the first step toward relief.* Accessed at www.psychologytoday.com/au/blog/experimentations/202007/5-keys-letting-go on March 21, 2024.

Bridges, W. (2004). *Transitions: Making sense of life's changes.* New York: Hachette.

Brown, B. (2010). *The gifts of imperfection: Let go of who you think you're supposed to be and embrace who you are.* Center City, MN: Hazelden.

Brown, B. (2022). *Atlas of the heart: Mapping meaningful connection and the language of human experience.* New York: Penguin Random House.

Bryant, D. A. (2019). Conditions that support middle leaders' work in organisational and system leadership: Hong Kong case studies. *School Leadership and Management, 39*(5), 415–433.

Bryk, A., & Schneider, B. (2002). *Trust in schools: A core resource for improvement.* New York: Russell Sage Foundation.

Burkeman, O. (2021). *Four thousand weeks: Time management for mortals.* New York: Farrar, Straus and Giroux.

Bush, T., & Glover, D. (2014). School leadership models: What do we know? *School Leadership and Management, 34*(5), 553–571.

Campbell, S. B., Halperin, J. M., & Sonuga-Barke, E. J. S. (2014). A developmental perspective on attention-deficit/hyperactivity disorder (ADHD). In M. Lewis & K. D. Rudolph (Eds.), *Handbook of developmental psychopathology* (3rd ed., pp. 427–448). New York: Springer.

Canfield, J. (n.d.). *Visualization techniques to manifest your dreams*. Accessed at https://jackcanfield.com/blog/visualize-and-affirm-your-desired-outcomes-a-step-by-step-guide on March 21, 2024.

Carden, J., Jones, R. J., & Passmore, J. (2022). Defining self-awareness in the context of adult development: A systematic literature review. *Journal of Management Education, 46*(1), 140–177.

Celestine, N. (2015, November 24). *How to change self-limiting beliefs according to psychology*. Accessed at https://positivepsychology.com/false-beliefs on March 21, 2024.

Center for Self-Determination Theory. (n.d.). *Theory*. Accessed at https://selfdeterminationtheory.org/theory on March 21, 2024.

Changing Works. (n.d.). *Socratic questions*. Accessed at http://changingminds.org/techniques/questioning/socratic_questions.htm on March 21, 2024.

CogniFit. (n.d.). *Cognitive shifting*. Accessed at www.cognifit.com/science/shifting on March 21, 2024.

Covey, S. R. (1989). *The seven habits of highly effective people*. New York: Free Press.

Cronkite, R. C., & Moos, R. H. (1995). Life context, coping processes, and depression. In E. E. Beckham & W. R. Leber (Eds.), *Handbook of depression* (2nd ed., pp. 569–587). New York: Guilford Press.

Danvers, J., De Blasio, H., & Grift, G. (2021). *Five ways of being: What learning leaders think, do, and say every day*. Bloomington, IN: Solution Tree Press.

Day, D. V., Fleenor, J. W., Atwater, L. E., Sturm, R. E., & McKee, R. A. (2014). Advances in leader and leadership development: A review of 25 years of research and theory. *Leadership Quarterly, 25*(1), 63–82. https://doi.org/10.1016/j.leaqua.2013.11.004

De Nobile, J. (2018). Towards a theoretical model of middle leadership in schools. *School Leadership and Management, 38*(4), 395–416.

Dijkstra, M. T. M., & Homan, A. C. (2016). Engaging in rather than disengaging from stress: Effective coping and perceived control. *Frontiers in Psychology, 7*, 1415.

DuFour, R., DuFour, R., Eaker, R., Many, T. W., Mattos, M., & Muhammad, A. (2024). *Learning by doing: A handbook for Professional Learning Communities at Work®* (4th ed.). Bloomington, IN: Solution Tree Press.

Dynamic Transitions. (n.d.). *The origins of impostor syndrome*. Accessed at www.dynamictransitionsllp.com/origins-imposter-syndrome on March 21, 2024.

Earley, P., & Bubb, S. (2004). *Leading and managing continuing professional development*. London: Paul Chapman.

Emergence. (n.d.). In *Vocabulary.com*. Accessed at www.vocabulary.com/dictionary/emergence on March 21, 2024.

Eurich, T. (2017). *Insight: The surprising truth about how others see us, how we see ourselves, and why the answers matter more than we think*. New York: Crown Business.

Eurich, T. (2018, January 4). *What self-awareness really is (and how to cultivate it): It's not just about introspection*. Accessed at https://hbr.org/2018/01/ what-self-awareness-really-is-and-how-to-cultivate-it on March 21, 2024.

Finn, K. (2021, February 10). *5 (sometimes harsh) realities you'll face when you finally decide to get real with yourself*. Accessed at www.yourtango.com/experts/drkarenfinn/truths-you-face-journey-deeper-self-awareness on March 21, 2024.

Flaum, J. P. (2010). *When it comes to business leadership, nice guys finish first*. Accessed at https://greenpeakpartners.com/wp-content/uploads/2018/09/Green-Peak_Cornell-University-Study_What-predicts-success.pdf on March 21, 2024.

Fogg, B. J. (2019). *Tiny habits: The small changes that change everything*. Boston: Houghton Mifflin Harcourt.

González, V. M., & Mark, G. (2004). Constant, constant, multi-tasking craziness: Managing multiple working spheres. In E. Dykstra-Erickson & M. Tscheligi (Eds.), *CHI '04: Proceedings of the SIGCHI Conference on Human Factors in Computing Systems* (pp. 113–120). New York: Association for Computing Machinery.

Grant, A. (2021). *Think again: The power of knowing what you don't know*. New York: Penguin.

Grootenboer, P., Rönnerman, K., & Edwards-Groves, C. (2017). Leading from the middle: A praxis-oriented practice. In P. Grootenboer, C. Edwards-Groves, & S. Choy (Eds.), *Practice theory perspectives on pedagogy and education: Praxis, diversity and contestation* (pp. 243–263). New York: Springer.

Gumus, S., Bellibas, M. S., Esen, M., & Gumus, E. (2018). A systematic review of studies on leadership models in educational research from 1980 to 2014. *Educational Management Administration & Leadership, 46*(1), 25–48. https://doi.org/10.1177/1741143216659296

Gurr, D. (2019). School middle leaders in Australia, Chile and Singapore. *School Leadership and Management, 39*(3–4), 278–296.

Hall, G., & Hord, S. (2011). *Implementing change: Patterns, principles, and potholes* (3rd ed.). Boston: Allyn and Bacon.

Hari, J. (2022). *Stolen focus: Why you can't pay attention—and how to think deeply again*. London: Bloomsbury.

Harvard Graduate School of Education. (2011). *Think, pair, share (adapted)*. Accessed at www.pz.harvard.edu/sites/default/files/Think%20Pair%20Share_2.pdf on March 21, 2024.

Harvard Health Publishing. (2021, February 15). *Protect your brain from stress.* Accessed at www.health.harvard.edu/mind-and-mood/protect-your-brain-from-stress on March 21, 2024.

Heffernan, A., Longmuir, F., Bright, D., & Kim, M. (2019). *Perceptions of teachers and teaching in Australia.* Clayton, Victoria, Australia: Monash University.

Howells, K. (2020). *Untangling you: How can I be grateful when I feel so resentful?* Elsternwick, Victoria, Australia: Major Street.

Influence. (n.d.). In *Merriam-Webster's online dictionary.* Accessed at www.merriam-webster.com/dictionary/influence on March 21, 2024.

Intégro Learning Company. (n.d.). *The D, i, S and C personality types.* Accessed at www.integro.com.au/the-disc-personality-types on March 21, 2024.

Jackson, P. W. (1990). *Life in classrooms* (Rev. ed.). New York: Teachers College Press.

Kegan, R. (1983). *The evolving self: Problem and process in human development.* Cambridge, MA: Harvard University Press.

Khema, A. (1987). *Being nobody, going nowhere: Meditations on the Buddhist path.* Somerville, MA: Wisdom.

Killgore, W. D. S. (2010). Effects of sleep deprivation on cognition. *Progress in Brain Research, 185,* 105–129.

Klein, A. (2021, December 6). *1,500 decisions a day (at least): How teachers cope with a dizzying array of questions.* Accessed at www.edweek.org/teaching-learning/1-500-decisions-a-day-at-least-how-teachers-cope-with-a-dizzying-array-of-questions/2021/12 on April 5, 2024.

Kolligian, J., Jr., & Sternberg, R. J. (1991). Perceived fraudulence in young adults: Is there an "imposter syndrome"? *Journal of Personality Assessment, 56*(2), 308–326.

Korn Ferry Institute. (2015, June 15). *Korn Ferry Institute study shows link between self-awareness and company financial performance.* Accessed at www.kornferry.com/about-us/press/korn-ferry-institute-study-shows-link-between-self-awareness-and-company-financial-performance on April 4, 2024.

Kouzes, J. (2009, January 26). *The origins of leadership.* Accessed at https://leadershipchallenge.typepad.com/leadership_challenge/2009/01/the-origins-of-leadership.html on March 21, 2024.

Lárusdóttir, S. H., & O'Connor, E. (2017). Distributed leadership and middle leadership practice in schools: A disconnect? *Irish Educational Studies, 36*(4), 423–438.

Leithwood, K., Harris, A., & Hopkins, D. (2020). Seven strong claims about successful school leadership revisited. *School Leadership and Management, 40*(1), 5–22.

LeJeune, C. (2007). *The worry trap: How to free yourself from worry and anxiety using acceptance and commitment therapy.* Oakland, CA: New Harbinger.

LePera, N. (2021). *How to do the work: Recognize your patterns, heal from your past, and create your self.* London: Orion Spring.

Lewis, C. S. (2001). *Mere Christianity.* New York: HarperCollins.

Lipscombe, K., De Nobile, J., Tindall-Ford, S., & Grice, C. (2020). *Formal middle leadership in NSW public schools: Full report.* Accessed at https://education.nsw.gov.au/content/dam/main-education/school-leadership-institute/mldp/FML_NSW_Research_Full_Report.pdf on March 21, 2024.

Lipscombe, K., Tindall-Ford, S., & Grootenboer, P. (2020). Middle leading and influence in two Australian schools. *Educational Management Administration and Leadership, 48*(6), 1063–1079. https://doi.org/10.1177/1741143219880324

Lipscombe, K., Tindall-Ford, S., & Lamanna, J. (2023). School middle leadership: A systematic review. *Educational Management Administration and Leadership, 51*(2), 270–288. Accessed at https://ro.uow.edu.au/cgi/viewcontent.cgi?article=1501&context=asshpapers on June 17, 2024.

Lovering, N. (2022). *Wanting to be liked is not the same as needing to be liked.* Accessed at https://psychcentral.com/blog/wanting-to-be-liked-is-not-the-same-as-needing-to-be-liked on March 21, 2024.

Lyubomirsky, S., King, L., & Diener, E. (2005). The benefits of frequent positive affect: Does happiness lead to success? *Psychological Bulletin, 131*(6), 803–855.

Madore, K. P., & Wagner, A. D. (2019). *Multicosts of multitasking.* Accessed at www.ncbi.nlm.nih.gov/pmc/articles/PMC7075496/ on April 16, 2024.

Martin, R. A., & Ford, T. E. (2018). *The psychology of humor: An integrative approach* (2nd ed.). Cambridge, MA: Academic Press.

Maslow, A. H. (1943). A theory of human motivation. *Psychological Review, 50*(4), 370–396.

Mayo Clinic. (2022, August 3). *Stress management.* Accessed at www.mayoclinic.org/healthy-lifestyle/stress-management/in-depth/exercise-and-stress/art-20044469 on April 19, 2024.

Miller, K. (2024, March 14). *Top 11 benefits of self-awareness according to science.* Accessed at https://positivepsychology.com/benefits-of-self-awareness on March 21, 2024.

MindTools. (n.d.). *Eisenhower's urgent/important principle: Using time effectively, not just efficiently.* Accessed at www.mindtools.com/pages/article/newHTE_91.htm on March 21, 2024.

Missimer, A. (2020, September 21). *Unlock the power of extreme focus: Wake up your reticular activating system.* Accessed at https://themovementparadigm.com/unlock-the-power-of-extreme-focus on March 21, 2024.

Moawad, T. (2020). *It takes what it takes: How to think neutrally and gain control of your life.* New York: HarperCollins.

Morad, N. (2017, September 28). *Part 1: How to be an adult—Kegan's theory of adult development.* Accessed at https://medium.com/@NataliMorad/how-to-be-an-adult-kegans-theory-of-adult-development-d63f4311b553 on March 21, 2024.

Morin, A. (2014). *13 things mentally strong people don't do: Take back your power, embrace change, face your fears, and train your brain for happiness and success.* New York: William Morrow.

Morin, A. (2018, September 14). *3 types of self-limiting beliefs that will keep you stuck in life (and what to do about them).* Accessed at www.inc.com/amy-morin/3-types-of-unhealthy-beliefs-that-will-drain-your-mental-strength-make-you-less-effective.html on March 21, 2024.

Nagoski, E., & Nagoski, A. (2019). *Burnout: The secret to unlocking the stress cycle.* New York: Ballantine.

Navarro, Z. (2006). In search of cultural interpretation of power: The contribution of Pierre Bourdieu. *IDS Bulletin, 37*(6), 11–22.

Neff, K. (2011). *Self-compassion: The proven power of being kind to yourself.* New York: William Morrow.

Pajares, M. F. (1992). Teachers' beliefs and educational research: Cleaning up a messy construct. *Review of Educational Research, 62*(3), 307–332.

Penley, J. A., Tomaka, J., & Wiebe, J. S. (2002). The association of coping to physical and psychological health outcomes: A meta-analytic review. *Journal of Behavioral Medicine, 25*(6), 551–603.

Reiners, B. (2023, February 23). *16 unconscious bias examples and how to avoid them in the workplace.* Accessed at https://builtin.com/diversity-inclusion/unconscious-bias-examples on March 21, 2024.

Riley, P. (2014). Principals' psychological health: It's not just lonely at the top, it's dangerous. *InPsych, 36*(6), 12.

Rowe, F. (2021). *Frank's 10:90 rule for conflict resolution.* Accessed at www.linkedin.com/pulse/franks-1090-rule-conflict-resolution-frank-rowe/ on April 19, 2024.

Sam, N. (n.d.). *Sociotropy.* Accessed at https://psychologydictionary.org/sociotropy on March 21, 2024.

Schmoker, M. (2004). Learning communities at the crossroads: Toward the best schools we've ever had. *Phi Delta Kappan, 86*(1), 84–88.

Sinclair, A. (2007). *Leadership for the disillusioned: Moving beyond myths and heroes to leading that liberates.* Crows Nest, NSW, Australia: Allen & Unwin.

Sloper, C., & Grift, G. (2021). *Collaborative teams that work: The definitive guide to cycles of learning in a PLC.* Bloomington, IN: Solution Tree Press.

Southwest Educational Development Laboratory. (n.d.). *Stages of concern.* Accessed at https://sedl.org/cbam/stages_of_concern.html on March 21, 2024.

Stanier, M. B. (2020, October 12). *Curiosity is a leadership superpower.* Accessed at https://dialoguereview.com/curiosity-is-a-leadership-superpower on March 21, 2024.

Suni, E. (2023, February 23). *Sleep hygiene: What it is, why it matters, and how to revamp your habits to get better nightly sleep.* Accessed at www.sleepfoundation.org/sleep-hygiene on March 21, 2024.

Takano, K., Sakamoto, S., & Tanno, Y. (2011). Ruminative and reflective forms of self-focus: Their relationships with interpersonal skills and emotional reactivity under interpersonal stress. *Personality and Individual Differences, 51*(4), 515–520. https://doi.org/10.1016/j.paid.2011.05.010

Tolle, E. (2004). *The power of now: A guide to spiritual enlightenment*. Novato, CA: New World Library.

Tseng, J., & Poppenk, J. (2020). Brain meta-state transitions demarcate thoughts across task contexts exposing the mental noise of trait neuroticism. *Nature Communications, 11*, 3480.

Wacquant, L. (2005). *Habitus*. In J. Beckert & M. Zafirovski (Eds.), *International encyclopedia of economic sociology* (p. 316). London: Routledge.

Wenner, J. A., & Campbell, T. (2017). The theoretical and empirical basis of teacher leadership: A review of the literature. *Review of Educational Research, 87*(1), 134–171.

Winterson, J. (1997). *Oranges are not the only fruit*. New York: Grove Press.

Yaribeygi, H., Panahi, Y., Sahraei, H., Johnston, T. P., & Sahebkar, A. (2017). The impact of stress on body function: A review. *EXCLI Journal, 16*, 1057–1072.

York-Barr, J., & Duke, K. (2004). What do we know about teacher leadership? Findings from two decades of scholarship. *Review of Educational Research, 74*(3), 255–316.

Index

NUMBERS

10/90 rule, 76

A

accepting tasks, 109
achievement, 20
adult development, complexities of, 123–124
advancement and pain points, 47–48
affinity biases, 65, 67. *See also* biases
American Psychological Association, 32
angry parent experience, 24–25
assumptions, 79, 121–123
attribution biases, 66, 67. *See also* biases
Aurelius, M., 78
avoidance coping, 72

B

Beck, J., 86, 89
beliefs. *See also* self-limiting beliefs
  beliefs about self, others, and the world, 90
  elements of the unconscious self and, 37, 38–39
benefits blueprints, 107
biases
  pinpointing your biases, 65–67
  relationships and, 32–33
Biradar, S., 120
boundaries, 63–64
breaking it down, 107
Brenner, G., 131
Brown, B., 119
building capacity, 3
Burkeman, O., 114–115

C

café conundrum experience, 27–28
calendars, 109
Campbell, T., 99
Carden, J., 15
change
  change fatigue, 69
  common pain points for middle leaders, 50
  as personal and inevitable, 82
  stages of, 82
chunking it up, 106–107

clarity and competence
- about, 9
- benefits of self-awareness, 19–21
- defining the self-aware middle leader, 11–19
- emerge exercises: the self-work, 21–22
- importance of clarity to competence, 9–11

cognitive boundaries, 63

cognitive restructuring, 91

collaboration
- dynamo's pain points and, 109
- lopsided collaboration, 56–58
- stages of concern, 125

Collaborative Teams That Work (Sloper and Grift), 10

collective attention, 101

common pain points for middle leaders. *See also* pain points
- about, 45
- desires, 48–49
- dreams, 47–48
- emerge exercises: the self-work, 53–54
- fears, 49–51
- frustrations, 51–52
- shifting sands and complexities of middle leadership, 45–52
- where to from here, 52–53

compassion
- compassion fatigue, 71
- demonstrating compassion, 126, 130

complaints and complaining, 75–76, 81

concern, stages of, 124–126

confirmation biases, 32, 65, 67. *See also* biases

conformity biases, 66, 67. *See also* biases

conscientiousness, 121, 122–123

conscious self, 16, 17, 28, 37, 65

creativity, 20

cultural factors, 52

D

death awareness, 83

decisions, 96, 97

delegating, expecting, and assuming, 107–108

demanding what's right, 126

depersonalization, 126, 127

desires and pain points, 48–49

Devarkar, V., 120

development, pain point for not appreciating the complexity of adult, 123–124

development, use of term, 37

Dhole, R., 120

difficult people, 117–118. *See also* judge and juror archetype

digital devices, 109, 111–112

dirty anxiety, 92

DiSC model, 121–123

disorganization, 104, 110–111

distress, 76–77

dominance, 121–122

dreams and pain points, 47–48

Duke, K., 12

dynamo archetype
- about, 99–100
- dynamo's pain points, 53, 103–105
- dynamo's pain points, self-awareness levers to overcome, 106–113
- emerge exercises: the self-work, 113–115
- slowing down to go fast, 100–113
- time as a problem, 100–102

E

Edwards-Groves, C., 13
egoic state, 18–19
Eisenhower matrix, 80, 112
elements of the unconscious self. *See* unconscious self
eliminating, automating, delegating, ideating, and concentrating, 107, 108
    emerge self-awareness model, 38
emergence, definition of, 7
emotional boundaries, 63
emotions, use of term, 39
empathy
    compassion and, 129, 130
    finding support, 81
    judge and juror's pain points and, 121, 123, 124, 126, 128–129
    self-awareness and, 20
entitlement, use of term, 39
escape coping, 72
Eurich, T., 42
eustress, 76

F

fairness, 126, 128
fatigue, 104, 110
fears
    common pain points for middle leaders, 49–51
    digging in to overcome the ostrich's pain points, 78–79
filter of perception, 18
focus. *See also* where to focus your self-awareness
    dynamo's pain points, 105, 111–112
    ostrich's pain points, 73–74
    time as a problem, 100–102

Four Thousand Weeks (Burkeman), 114–115
frame of reference, enlarging, 81–82
frustrations and pain points, 51–52
fulfillment and pain points, 49

G

Grift, G., 10
Grootenboer, P., 13
growth, use of term, 37

H

habit change, 20
habitus, 65
hardships as opportunities for growth
    learning from experience, 24–28
    people as enablers of our self-awareness, 29–33
    role of self-awareness, 28–29
Hari, J., 105
headphones, 111
hidden curriculum, x
high need and low need, 112–113

I

I can't be bothered pain points, 103, 106
impact and pain points, 48–49
imposter archetype
    about, 85–86
    emerge exercises: the self-work, 97–98
    imposter's pain points, 53, 89–90
    imposter's pain points, self-awareness levers to overcome, 90–96
    two words: "I'm enough," 87–89
    voice within, 86–96
imposter syndrome, 50, 86
influence, 13, 121, 122

inspiration and pain points, 49
intention, it's not all about you, 61–62
introduction
    leadership as personal, 1–4
    this book and how to use it, 4–7
it can wait pain point, 103, 106–107
it's not good enough pain point, 105, 112–113

J

Jadhav, B., 120
Jones, R., 15
joy, pain point for loss of, 60
judge and juror archetype
    about, 117–118
    difficult Diane, 118–120
    emerge exercises: the self-work, 131–132
    judge and juror's pain points, 53, 120–126
    judge and juror's pain points, self-awareness levers to overcome, 126–131
    taking a different look, 118–131

K

keeping, trashing, or flinging, 110–111

L

Lamanna, J., 12
leadership. *See also* middle leaders
    definition of, 11
    leadership dedication, xi–xii
    leadership retreat planning t-chart, 113
    my love affair with teaching and leading, ix–xi
    as personal, 1–4

learning and pain points, 47
letting go, 127, 131
Lewis, C., 90
lightening up, 83
Lipscombe, K., 12, 14
loss of joy pain points, 60

M

Madore, K., 104
management
    breaking it down to overcome the ostrich's pain points, 79–80
    self-management, 72
    stages of concern, 125
    time management, 63
mental states, 37, 38, 39–40
Merriam-Webster, 13
middle leaders. *See also* common pain points for middle leaders; leadership
    about, 12–15
    defining the self-aware middle leader, 11–19
    dual role of, xiii
mindfulness, 18–19
Morad, N., 123
motivations
    elements of the unconscious self and, 37, 42
    emerge self-awareness model, 38
    ostrich's pain points, 74–75
multitasking, 104

N

negativity and neutrality, 64–65
neutral zone, 82
no-disruption time, 111

not appreciating the complexity of adult development pain point, 123–124

not understanding that people come before process pain point, 124–126

not understanding your people pain point, 121–123

O

ostrich archetype
- about, 69
- emerge exercises: the self-work, 84
- impossible student and, 71–72
- ostrich's pain points, 53, 72–77
- ostrich's pain points, self-awareness levers to overcome, 77–83
- rolling with it, 69–83

others' perceptions, 37, 38, 42–43

out of depth, pain point for feelings of, 76–77

P

pain points. *See also* common pain points for middle leaders
- about, 23
- archetypes of, 53. *See also specific archetypes*
- awareness and, 6–7
- emerge exercises: the self-work, 33–34
- hardships as opportunities for growth, 24–33
- from pain point to opportunity, 35–37

pain points and people: agents of self-awareness. *See* pain points

painting a mental picture, 95–96, 97

Passmore, J., 15

patience, 127, 130–131

peer pressure, 66

perceptions, 18, 37, 38, 42–43

perfectionism, 105, 112–113

personal boundaries, 63

personal characteristics, 52

personality traits, 37, 38, 41

perspective taking, 20

phones, 109, 111–112

physiological responses, 37, 38, 40–41

pleaser archetype
- about, 55
- dynamo's pain points and, 104
- emerge exercises: the self-work, 67–68
- lopsided collaboration, 56–58
- pleaser's pain points, 53, 58–60
- pleaser's pain points, self-awareness levers to overcome, 60–67
- rainy hearts, 56–67

priorities
- dynamo's pain points, 105, 112
- ostrich's pain points, 79–80

procrastination, 103, 106–107

professional learning communities (PLCs), 10

pup I was sold experience, 25–27

R

rapport, 126, 127–128

reactions, unconscious reactions and conscious responses, 30–31

regulating and delegating, 80–81

relationships
- common pain points for middle leaders, 50–51, 51–52
- deepening relationships and understanding differences, 32–33
- self-awareness and, 20

relief theory, 130

resentment pain points, 59–60

responses, unconscious reactions and conscious responses, 30–31

rewards, 106
Rönnerman, K., 13

S

seeking support, 80–81
self-awareness. *See also* where to focus your self-awareness
    about, 15–17
    benefits of, 19–21
    definition of, 7
    emerge self-awareness model, 38
    focusing your, 37–43
    pain points and people: agents of self-awareness. *See* pain points
    people as enablers of our, 29–33
    role of in opportunities for growth, 28–29
    self-awareness levers to overcome the dynamo's pain points, 106–113
    self-awareness levers to overcome the imposter's pain points, 90–96
    self-awareness levers to overcome the ostrich's pain points, 77–83
    self-awareness levers to overcome the pleaser's pain points, 60–67
    self-knowledge, self-consciousness, and mindfulness and, 18–19
self-care pain points, 59
self-consciousness, 18
self-esteem, 20
self-knowledge, 18
self-limiting beliefs. *See also* imposter archetype
    about, 85–86
    common pain points for middle leaders, 50
    pausing and identifying, 91–92, 97
    thought worms, 89
self-regulation, 20, 126, 129
self-stories, 92–93, 97

self-worth, 63
similarity biases, 65. *See also* biases
Sinclair, A., 14
sleep, 110
Sloper, C., 10
sociotropy, 58
Socratic questioning, 92
stages of concern, 124–126
Stanier, M., 123
steadiness, 121, 122
stimuli attention, 73
Stolen Focus: Why You Can't Pay Attention (Hari), 105
stories, self-stories, 92–93, 97
stress
    fatigue and sleep deprivation, 104
    focus and, 74
    out of depth, pain point for feeling, 76–77
structural factors, 52
support networks, 80–81, 126, 130
suspending judgement, 64, 81, 118, 120. *See also* judge and juror archetype
sustained attention, 73

T

taking stock and pain points, 109
teacher leadership, use of term, 12. *See also* middle leaders
think, pair, share activity, 10
thought worms, 89
thoughts, use of term, 39
time
    dynamo's pain points, 103–104, 107–109
    middle leaders and, 51, 52
    as a problem, 100–102
    time boundaries, 63–64
Tindall-Ford, S., 12

toward action template, 114

trust, 32, 33, 119, 120

U

unconscious self. *See also* conscious self

    elements of the unconscious self, 37–43

    pinpointing your biases and, 65–66

    self-awareness and, 15, 16, 17

    unconscious reactions and conscious responses, 30–31

V

values

    beliefs and, 38

    digging in to overcome the ostrich's pain points, 78–79

    elements of the unconscious self and, 37, 39

    emerge self-awareness model, 38

visualization, painting a mental picture, 95–96, 97

W

Wagner, A., 104

wants and needs, differences between, 62–63

well-being and pain points, 47

Wenner, J., 99

what-ifs, 93–95, 97

where to focus your self-awareness. *See also* self-awareness

    about, 35

    emerge exercises: the self-work, 43–44

    focusing your self-awareness, 37–43

    from pain point to opportunity, 35–37

Y

York-Barr, J., 12

Z

zeroing in, 106

Transformative Collaboration
Tonia Flanagan, Gavin Grift, Kylie Lipscombe, Colin Sloper, and Janelle Wills
Dive deep into one of the strongest strategies for school improvement—the PLC process. You will explore five collaboration-based commitments—from gaining clarity to building trust—that will help you build a PLC that provides the best possible avenues of learning to students.
BKB017

Collaborative Teams That Work
Colin Sloper and Gavin Grift
Collaborative Teams That Work is the ultimate guide to excellent collaboration. Rely on this resource as you set up collaborative teams within your PLC, and then refer back to it before, during, and after meetings to maintain focus on the right work.
BKB012

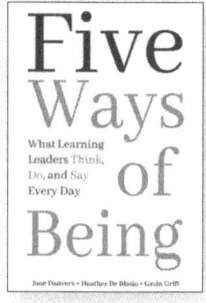

Five Ways of Being
Jane Danvers, Heather De Blasio, and Gavin Grift
In this must-read guide, the authors challenge and reinvent the mindset of leadership. Each chapter outlines one of five ways of being—from forming trusting relationships to being purposeful in thought and action—that will empower you to genuinely lead learning in staff, colleagues, and students.
BKB013

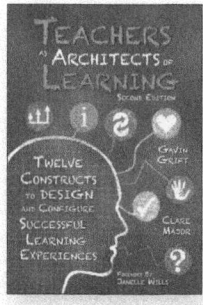

Teachers as Architects of Learning (Second Edition)
Gavin Grift and Clare Major
Craft a personal blueprint for teaching that ensures student learning stands as the foundation of your classroom. Drawing on research from the field and the authors' professional experience, this resource guides educators in building their wisdom around the art of teaching.
BKB010

Visit SolutionTree.com or call 800.733.6786 to order.

"Tremendous, tremendous, tremendous!

The speaker made me do some very deep internal reflection about the **PLC process** and the personal responsibility I have in making the school improvement process work for ALL kids."

—Marc Rodriguez, teacher effectiveness coach, Denver Public Schools, Colorado

PD Services

Our experts draw from decades of research and their own experiences to bring you practical strategies for building and sustaining a high-performing PLC. You can choose from a range of customizable services, from a one-day overview to a multiyear process.

Book your PLC PD today!
888.763.9045

Solution Tree